A CHOICE OF D

G000151401

A CHOICE OF

Dryden's
verse

SELECTED AND WITH AN INTRODUCTION BY

W. H. Auden

FABER AND FABER
3 QUEEN SQUARE
LONDON

First published in 1973
by Faber and Faber Limited
3 Queen Square, London WC1
Printed in Great Britain by
Unwin Brothers Limited, Old Woking
All rights reserved

ISBN 0 571 10255 7
(Faber Paper Covered Editions)

ISBN 0 571 10238 7
(hard bound edition)

CONTENTS

In a volume of this size it is clearly impossible to give an adequate representation of the whole range of Dryden's literary activities. I began, therefore, by deciding to ignore his plays. In my opinion, despite some fine rhetorical speeches, they are rather boring. The conventions and style of French Classical Tragedy on which they are modelled do not, I believe, suit either the English language or the English sensibility. What translations of Racine or Corneille have really been successful? The Restoration dramas which have survived are comedies in prose like those of Congreve and Wycherley. Then, for all the time he spent writing plays, I do not think Dryden was by nature a playwright, because he cannot create imaginary characters in whom one can believe. His imagination was only genuinely aroused by historical reality, friends and enemies whom he knew personally, events of which he had first-hand knowledge. Then I have excluded his 'translations' in the strict sense. As for his translation of the *Aeneid*, I agree with C. S. Lewis that it is too 'classical', that Gavin Douglas' translation is nearer to what Virgil must have sounded like to his contemporaries. Pope's *Iliad* is also too 'classical' to be Homeric, but it is a much finer English poem. The *Fables* are another matter, for in them Dryden makes no claim to be translating Chaucer or Ovid or Boccaccio. He writes his own poem as an 'imitation after the manner of'. Lastly, with the greatest regret, I felt that there was no room to include any of his prose criticism, though this is of the highest historical and aesthetic importance.

Dryden's lifetime (1631–1700) coincided with the most violent and revolutionary changes in political, religious and social life which England has so far experienced. When he was born, Charles I claimed to rule by Divine Right: then came the Civil War, Charles' execution, the Protectorate, The Restoration and, finally, the 'Glorious Revolution' of 1688. In such a period it must always be a temptation for the average citizen, and particularly for one of Dryden's temperament, to support whichever side seems to be winning and to desert it when it seems to be a lost cause, and, in his youth, Dryden does seem to have been a bit of a time-server. His readiness to write a panegyric on Cromwell and two years later a panegyric on Charles II is a little disturbing. I am quite convinced, however, that his conversion to Roman Catholicism was not, as Macaulay believed, a worldly act, but perfectly genuine. He must have known that, even if James II succeeded in abolishing the political and educational disabilities imposed on Roman Catholics, there was not the remotest chance of the Anglican Church, still less of the Dissenters, rejoining the Catholic Fold.

Any persecution of Protestants, as under Queen Mary, was out of the question. From a worldly point of view, he would have had nothing to fear either from the State or from his public, had he remained an Anglican. In fact, as we know, James was overthrown and Dryden lost his Poet Laureateship.

In discussing Dryden as a poet, I am painfully aware that anything I say can only be a feeble echo of Professor Mark Van Doren's magnificent study. When I was an undergraduate, most of my elders, I think, still agreed with Matthew Arnold's dictum: "Dryden and Pope are classics of our Prose." Such a view is, I hope outmoded, but, in approaching the work of any poet, it is essential that a reader should not expect from him a kind of poetry which he cannot write and, usually, does not want to. Dryden, for example, has no imaginative insight into violent personal emotions, such as sexual love. Though he takes an interest in cosmological theories like that of Lucretius, he shows no concern for non-human nature in the Wordsworthian sense. Nor can one imagine him having any kind of mystical experience like Traherne or Blake. His attempts at what the Metaphysical poets called Wit are seldom successful, as is evidenced by many stanzas in *Annus Mirabilis*, e.g:

> *On high-rais'd decks the haughty Belgians ride,*
> *Beneath whose shade our humble frigates go :*
> *Such port the elephant bears, and so defied*
> *By the rhinoceros, her unequal foe.*

The *Stuffed Owl* printed Stanza V of *Threnodia Augustalis* as an example of bad, because unintentionally comic, verse.

> *. . . Like helpless friends who view from shore*
> *The labouring ship, and hear the tempest roar ;*

> *So stood they with their arms across*
> *Not to assist, but to deplore*
> *Th' inevitable loss.*

Here I disagree: I think Dryden meant to be funny. Lastly, he lacks what I would call Fantasy. He could not, for example, have written these lines by Pope:

> *Here living Teapots stand, one arm held out,*
> *One bent; the Handle this, and that the Spout:*
> *A Pipkin there like Homer's Tripod walks;*
> *Here sighs a Jar and there a Goose-pye talks.*
> *Men prove with Child, as powr'ful Fancy works,*
> *And Maids turn'd Bottles, call aloud for Corks.*

On the other hand Dryden is pre-eminent in English Literature as the poet of Common Sense. His lines have no undertones, as Pope's often have: they mean exactly what, on first reading, they seem to say. He is the ideal poet to read when one is weary, as I often am, of Poetry with a capital P, the mannerisms and obscurities of the symbolists, the surrealists and their ilk.

His literary Godfather was, of course, Ben Jonson, but his real ancestor, in my opinion, is Dunbar. Both of them thought of themselves as professional 'makars' of verbal objects, whose imagination was excited by actual occasions, almost any occasion and Dryden is, without any doubt, the greatest Occasional Poet in English.

He does not 'rise' to the occasion: he elevates it. Whether he is eulogising or satirising, events and persons that in real life may have been unimportant are transfigured by his verse into events and persons that really matter to the reader. Dryden is also the master of argument in verse. The extracts in this volume from *Religio Laici* and *The Hind and the Panther* will, I hope, give some idea of his powers of ratiocination, but they are inadequate: both poems should be read *in toto*. When one compares them with Pope's exercise in argument, *The Essay on Man*, Dryden's superiority is immediately apparent. One reason for this is that his subject matter is more interesting than Pope's but the main reason is, I believe, that, while both employ the end-stopped couplet, Pope tends to think in terms of single couplets, while Dryden thinks in terms of paragraphs.

In Dryden's day there was competition between two kinds of rhymed decasyllabics, the end-stopped couplet developed by Waller and Cowley, and the enjambed couplet, an extreme example of which are the *Satires* of Donne.

> *Graius stays still at home here, and because*
> *Some preachers, vile ambitious bawds and laws,*
> *Still new, like fashions, bid him think that she*
> *Which dwells with us, is only perfect, he*
> *Embraceth her, whom his godfathers will*
> *Tender to him, being tender; as wards will*
> *Take such wives as their guardians will offer, or*
> *Pay values. Careless Phrygius doth abhor*
> *All, because all cannot be good: as one,*
> *Knowing some women whores, dares marry none.*

Though Dryden sometimes uses enjambement, he does so very sparingly, and the example he set made the end-stopped couplet the standard verse medium for non-lyrical poems of any length for over a century. When one compares his couplet with Pope's, one notices that he is much freer in his distribution of accents. Pope believed that a pause should always be made after either the fourth or the fifth or the sixth syllable, so that his lines almost always break into two halves, complementary or antithetical. Dryden, influenced perhaps by blank verse, knows no such limitations. His pauses may come anywhere and often they do not come at all. E.g.:

> *Drawn to the dregs of a democracy*
> ***
> *Of the true old enthusiastic breed.*
> ***
> *To the next headlong steep of anarchy*
> ***
> *But baffled by an arbitrary crowd*

Like all poets, both of them make use of alliteration for

reasons of sound and sense, but Dryden's use of it is much more conspicuous than Pope's.

> *In friendship false, implacable in hate,*
> *Resolved to ruin or to rule the state;*
> *****
>
> *And pricks up his predestinating ears*
> *****
>
> *This general worship is to praise and pray,*
> *One part to borrow blessings, one to pay;*

Pope disapproved of using an alexandrine to make a triplet. Dryden employs it, but with discretion and always to good effect.

> *Firm* Dorique *Pillars found your solid Base:*
> *The Fair* Corinthian *Crowns the higher Space;*
> *Thus all below is Strength, and all above is Grace.*
> *****
>
> *What Help from Arts Endeavours can we have!*
> Guibbons *but guesses, nor is sure to save:*
> *But* Maurus *sweeps whole Parishes, and Peoples ev'ry Grave*

If Dryden's songs are not as prosodically interesting or as varied in theme as those of the Elizabethans, like Campion and the anonymous madrigal poets, this is not altogether his fault. What composers, except Purcell, were there in his time to write for? Aside from the Odes for music, most of his songs are Light Verse, but all of them are settable, sometimes perhaps, too easily so.

Had I been compiling this selection simply for my own amusement, I might well have printed all his Prologues and Epilogues and nothing else. In them, as in few poems, one hears the speaking voice, neither too soft nor too loud, of a civilised man, defending the cause of civilisation both in social manners and in the Arts. I suspect that those who deny that Dryden is a poet believe that all poems should 'sing'. I don't agree.

Let George Saintsbury have the last word.

One feels, however much one may worship the earlier Caroline fancy and the later Romantic imagination—however conscious one may be that Dryden is not Blake or Coleridge, Shelley or Keats, Tennyson or even Browning—a sort of indignation at having to apologise in any way for him. We may with him, prosodically as well as poetically, as a whole be on Earth and not in Heaven. But (as Browning has been mentioned) his Earth is so good that it seems a little impertinent, and more than a little ungracious, to inquire, while we are on it, whether Heaven is not best.

W. H. AUDEN

TO MY HONOUR'D FRIEND SIR ROBERT HOWARD, ON HIS
EXCELLENT POEMS

As there is music uninform'd by art
In those wild notes, which, with a merry heart,
The birds in unfrequented shades express,
Who, better taught at home, yet please us less:
So in your verse a native sweetness dwells,
Which shames composure, and its art excels.
Singing no more can your soft numbers grace
Then paint adds charms unto a beauteous face.
Yet as, when mighty rivers gently creep,
Their even calmness does suppose them deep;
Such is your Muse: no metaphor swell'd high
With dangerous boldness lifts her to the sky:
Those mounting fancies, when they fall again,
Shew sand and dirt at bottom do remain.
So firm a strength, and yet withal so sweet,
Did never but in Samson's riddle meet.
'T is strange each line so great a weight should bear,
And yet no sign of toil, no sweat appear.
Either your art hides art, as Stoics feign
Then least to feel, when most they suffer pain;
And we, dull souls, admire, but cannot see
What hidden springs within the engine be;
Or 't is some happiness that still pursues
Each act and motion of your graceful Muse.
Or is it fortune's work, that in your head
The curious net* that is for fancies spread,
Lets thro' its meshes every meaner thought,
While rich ideas there are only caught?
Sure that's not all: this is a piece too fair
To be the child of chance, and not of care.
No atoms casually together hurl'd
Could e'er produce so beautiful a world.
Nor dare I such a doctrine here admit,
As would destroy the providence of wit.

*Rete mirabile.

‡13‡

'T is your strong genius then which does not feel
Those weights would make a weaker spirit reel.
To carry weight, and run so lightly too,
Is what alone your Pegasus can do.
Great Hercules himself could ne'er do more,
Than not to feel those heav'ns and gods he bore.
Your easier odes, which for delight were penn'd,
Yet our instruction make their second end:
We're both enrich'd and pleas'd, like them that woo
At once a beauty and a fortune too.
Of moral knowledge Poesy was queen,
And still she might, had wanton wits not been;
Who, like ill guardians, liv'd themselves at large,
And, not content with that, debauch'd their charge.
Like some brave captain, your successful pen
Restores the exil'd to her crown again;
And gives us hope, that having seen the days
When nothing flourish'd but fanatic bays,
All will at length in this opinion rest:
"A sober prince's government is best."
This is not all; your art the way has found
To make improvement of the richest ground,
That soil which those immortal laurels bore,
That once the sacred Maro's temples wore.
Elisa's griefs are so express'd by you,
They are too eloquent to have been true.
Had she spoke, Æneas had obey'd
What Dido, rather then what Jove, had said.
If funeral rites can give a ghost repose,
Your muse so justly has discharged those,
Elisa's shade may now its wand'ring cease,
And claim a title to the fields of peace.
But if Æneas be oblig'd, no less
Your kindness great Achilles doth confess;
Who, dress'd by Statius in too bold a look,
Did ill become those virgin's robes he took.
To understand how much we owe to you,
We must your numbers with your author's view;
Then we shall see his work was lamely rough,

Each figure stiff, as if design'd in buff;
His colours laid so thick on every place,
As only shew'd the paint, but hid the face.
But as in perspective we beauties see,
Which in the glass, not in the picture, be;
So here our sight obligingly mistakes
That wealth which his your bounty only makes.
Thus vulgar dishes are by cooks disguis'd,
More for their dressing than their substance priz'd.
Your curious notes** so search into that age,
When all was fable but the sacred page,
That, since in that dark night we needs must stray,
We are at least misled in pleasant way.
But what we most admire, your verse no less
The prophet than the poet doth confess.
Ere our weak eyes discern'd the doubtful streak
Of light, you saw great Charles his morning break.
So skilful seamen ken the land from far,
Which shews like mists to the dull passenger.
To Charles your Muse first pays her duteous love,
As still the ancients did begin from Jove.
With Monk you end, whose name preserv'd shall be,
As Rome recorded Rufus' memory,***
Who thought it greater honor to obey
His country's interest than the world to sway.
But to write worthy things of worthy men,
Is the peculiar talent of your pen:
Yet let me take your mantle up, and I
Will venture in your right to prophesy.

"This work, by merit first of fame secure,
Is likewise happy in its geniture:
For, since 't is born when Charles ascends the throne,
It shares at once his fortune and its own."

**Annotations on Statius.*
***Hic situs est Rufus, qui pulso Vindice quondam, Imperium asseruit non sibi sed patriæ.*

from THE INDIAN QUEEN
SONG IS SUPPOS'D SUNG BY AERIAL SPIRITS

> Poor mortals that are clogg'd with earth below
>> Sink under love and care,
>> While we that dwell in air
> Such heavy passions never know.
>> Why then should mortals be
>> Unwilling to be free
>> From blood, that sullen cloud
>> Which shining souls does shroud?
>>> Then they'll shew bright,
>>> And like us light,
> When leaving bodies with their care,
>> They slide to us and air.

from THE INDIAN EMPEROR
SONG BY AN INDIAN WOMAN

I   Ah fading joy, how quickly art thou past!
        Yet we thy ruin haste.
    As if the cares of human life were few,
        We seek out new:
    And follow fate, which would too fast pursue.

II   See how on every bough the birds express
        In their sweet notes their happiness.
    They all enjoy, and nothing spare;
    But on their mother Nature lay their care:
    Why then should man, the lord of all below,
        Such troubles choose to know,
    As none of all his subjects undergo?

III Hark, hark, the waters fall, fall, fall,
    And with a murmuring sound
    Dash, dash upon the ground,
        To gentle slumbers call.

178   Now, anchors weigh'd, the seamen shout so shrill,
          That heav'n, and earth, and the wide ocean rings;
      A breeze from westward waits their sails to fill,
          And rests in those high beds his downy wings.

179   The wary Dutch this gathering storm foresaw,
          And durst not bide it on the English coast:
      Behind their treach'rous shallows they withdraw,
          And there lay snares to catch the British host.

180   So the false spider, when her nets are spread,
          Deep ambush'd in her silent den does lie,
      And feels far off the trembling of her thread,
          Whose filmy cord should bind the struggling fly;

181   Then, if at last she find him fast beset,
          She issues forth, and runs along her loom:
      She joys to touch the captive in her net,
          And drags the little wretch in triumph home.

182   The Belgians hop'd that, with disorder'd haste,
          Our deep-cut keels upon the sands might run;
      Or, if with caution leisurely were pass'd,
          Their numerous gross might charge us one by one.

183   But with a fore-wind pushing them above,
          And swelling tide that heav'd them from below,
      O'er the blind flats our warlike squadrons move,
          And with spread sails to welcome battle go.

184   It seem'd as there the British Neptune stood,
          With all his hosts of waters at command,
      Beneath them to submit th' officious flood,
          *And with his trident shov'd them off the sand.

Levat ipse tridenti, Et vastas aperit syrtes, &c.—VIRG.

185   To the pale foes they suddenly draw near,
        And summon them to unexpected fight;
    They start like murderers when ghosts appear,
        And draw their curtains in the dead of night.

186   Now van to van the foremost squadrons meet,
Second The midmost battles hast'ning up behind;
battle Who view, far off, the storm of falling sleet,
        And hear their thunder rattling in the wind.

187   At length the adverse admirals appear;
        (The two bold champions of each country's right:)
    Their eyes describe the lists as they come near,
        And draw the lines of death before they fight.

188   The distance judg'd for shot of every size,
        The linstocks touch, the pond'rous ball expires:
    The vig'rous seaman every porthole plies,
        And adds his heart to every gun he fires.

189   Fierce was the fight on the proud Belgians' side,
        For honour, which they seldom sought before;
    But now they by their own vain boasts were tied,
        And forc'd at least in shew to prize it more.

190   But sharp remembrance on the English part,
        And shame of being match'd by such a foe,
    Rouse conscious virtue up in every heart,
        **And seeming to be stronger makes them so.

191   Nor long the Belgians could that fleet sustain,
        Which did two gen'rals' fates, and Cæsar's bear:
    Each several ship a victory did gain,
        As Rupert or as Albemarle were there.

192   Their batter'd admiral too soon withdrew,
        Unthank'd by ours for his unfinish'd fight;
    But he the minds of his Dutch masters knew,
        Who call'd that providence which we call'd flight.

**Possunt, quia posse videntur.*—Virg.

193   Never did men more joyfully obey,
      Or sooner understand the sign to fly:
   With such alacrity they bore away,
      As if to praise them all the States stood by.

PROLOGUES *to* SECRET LOVE

PROLOGUE

I   He who writ this, not without pains and thought
   From French and English theatres has brought
   Th' exactest rules by which a play is wrought:

II   The unities of action, place, and time;
   The scenes unbroken; and a mingled chime
   Of Jonson's humour with Corneille's rhyme.

III   But while dead colours he with care did lay,
   He fears his wit or plot he did not weigh,
   Which are the living beauties of a play.

IV   Plays are like towns, which, howe'er fortified
   By engineers, have still some weaker side
   By the o'er-seen defendant unespied.

V   And with that art you make approaches now;
   Such skilful fury in assaults you show,
   That every poet without shame may bow.

VI   Ours therefore humbly would attend your doom,
   If, soldier-like, he may have terms to come
   With flying colours and with beat of drum.

[*The* PROLOGUE *goes out, and stays while a tune is play'd, after which he returns again.*

SECOND PROLOGUE

   I had forgot one half, I do protest,
   And now am sent again to speak the rest.
   He bows to every great and noble wit;
   But to the little Hectors of the pit

Our poet's sturdy, and will not submit.
He'll be beforehand with 'em, and not stay
To see each peevish critic stab his play:
Each puny censor, who, his skill to boast,
Is cheaply witty on the poet's cost.
No critic's verdict should of right stand good;
They are excepted all, as men of blood;
And the same law should shield him from their fury
Which has excluded butchers from a jury.
You'd all be wits—
But writing's tedious, and that way may fail;
The most compendious method is to rail;
Which you so like, you think yourselves ill us'd
When in smart prologues you are not abus'd.
A civil prologue is approv'd by no man;
You hate it as you do a civil woman:
Your fancy's pall'd, and liberally you pay
To have it quicken'd, ere you see a play;
Just as old sinners, worn from their delight,
Give money to be whipp'd to appetite.
But what a pox keep I so much ado
To save our poet? He is one of you;
A brother judgment, and, as I hear say,
A cursed critic as e'er damn'd a play.
Good salvage gentlemen, your own kind spare;
He is, like you, a very wolf or bear.
Yet think not he'll your ancient rights invade,
Or stop the course of your free damning trade;
For he, he vows, at no friend's play can sit,
But he must needs find fault to shew his wit.
Then, for his sake, ne'er stint your own delight;
Throw boldly, for he sets to all that write:
With such he ventures on an even lay,
For they bring ready money into play.
Those who write not, and yet all writers nick,
Are bankrupt gamesters, for they damn on tick.

SONG *from* SECRET LOVE

I I feed a flame within, which so torments me,
   That it both pains my heart, and yet contents me:
   'T is such a pleasing smart, and I so love it,
   That I had rather die then once remove it.

II Yet he for whom I grieve shall never know it;
    My tongue does not betray, nor my eyes show it:
    Not a sigh, nor a tear, my pain discloses,
    But they fall silently, like dew on roses.

III Thus to prevent my love from being cruel,
     My heart's the sacrifice, as 't is the fuel:
     And while I suffer this, to give him quiet,
     My faith rewards my love, tho' he deny it.

IV On his eyes will I gaze, and there delight me;
    Where I conceal my love, no frown can fright me:
    To be more happy, I dare not aspire;
    Nor can I fall more low, mounting no higher.

EPILOGUE *to* THE TEMPEST

          Gallants, by all good signs it does appear
          That sixty-seven's a very damning year,
          For knaves abroad, and for ill poets here.

          Among the Muses there's a gen'ral rot:
          The rhyming Mounsieur and the Spanish plot,
          Defy or court, all's one, they go to pot.

          The ghosts of poets walk within this place,
          And haunt us actors wheresoe'er we pass,
          In visions bloodier than King Richard's was.

          For this poor wretch he has not much to say,
          But quietly brings in his part o' th' play,
          And begs the favour to be damn'd to-day.

He sends me only like a sh'riff's man here,
To let you know the malefactor's near,
And that he means to die *en cavalier.*

For if you should be gracious to his pen,
Th' example will prove ill to other men,
And you'll be troubled with 'em all again.

EPILOGUE *to* TYRANNIC LOVE
Spoken by Mrs. Ellen, when she was to be carried off dead by the bearers.

[*To the Bearer.*

Hold, are you mad? you damn'd confounded dog,
I am to rise, and speak the epilogue.

[*To the Audience.*

I come, kind gentlemen, strange news to tell ye,
I am the ghost of poor departed Nelly.
Sweet ladies, be not frighted, I'll be civil;
I'm what I was, a little harmless devil:
For after death, we sprites have just such natures
We had for all the world, when human creatures;
And therefore I that was an actress here,
Play all my tricks in hell, a goblin there.
Gallants, look to 't, you say there are no sprites;
But I'll come dance about your beds at nights.
And faith you'll be in a sweet kind of taking,
When I surprise you between sleep and waking.
To tell you true, I walk because I die
Out of my calling in a tragedy.
O poet, damn'd dull poet, who could prove
So senseless! to make Nelly die for love!
Nay, what's yet worse, to kill me in the prime
Of Easter term, in tart and cheese-cake time!
I'll fit the fop, for I'll not one word say
T' excuse his godly out-of-fashion play:
A play, which if you dare but twice sit out,
You'll all be slander'd, and be thought devout.

But farewell, gentlemen, make haste to me;
I'm sure ere long to have your company.
As for my epitaph, when I am gone,
I'll trust no poet, but will write my own:

Here Nelly lies, who, tho' she liv'd a slattern,
Yet died a princess, acting in St. Cathar'n.

SONG *from* AN EVENING'S LOVE

I   Calm was the even, and clear was the sky,
    And the new-budding flowers did spring,
When all alone went Amyntas and I
    To hear the sweet nightingale sing.
I sate, and he laid him down by me,
    But scarcely his breath he could draw;
For when with a fear, he began to draw near,
    He was dash'd with: "A ha ha ha ha!"

II   He blush'd to himself, and lay still for a while,
    And his modesty curb'd his desire;
But straight I convinc'd all his fear with a smile,
    Which added new flames to his fire.
"O Sylvia," said he, "you are cruel,
    To keep your poor lover in awe;"
Then once more he press'd with his hand to my breast,
    But was dash'd with: "A ha ha ha ha!"

III   I knew 't was his passion that caus'd all his fears,
    And therefore I pitied his case;
I whisper'd him softly: "There's nobody near,"
    And laid my cheek close to his face:
But as he grew bolder and bolder,
    A shepherd came by us and saw,
And just as our bliss we began with a kiss,
    He laugh'd out with: "A ha ha ha ha!"

PROLOGUE

Our author, by experience, finds it true,
'T is much more hard to please himself than you;
And out of no feign'd modesty, this day
Damns his laborious trifle of a play:
Not that it's worse than what before he writ,
But he has now another taste of wit;
And, to confess a truth, (tho' out of time,)
Grows weary of his long-lov'd mistress, Rhyme.
Passion's too fierce to be in fetters bound,
And nature flies him like enchanted ground.
What verse can do, he has perform'd in this,
Which he presumes the most correct of his;
But spite of all his pride, a secret shame
Invades his breast at Shakespeare's sacred name:
Aw'd when he hears his godlike Romans rage,
He, in just despair, would quit the stage;
And to an age less polish'd more unskill'd,
Does, with disdain, the foremost honours yield.
As with the greater dead he dares not strive,
He would not match his verse with those who live:
Let him retire, betwixt two ages cast,
The first of this, and hindmost of the last.
A losing gamester, let him sneak away;
He bears no ready money from the play.
The fate which governs poets thought it fit
He should not raise his fortunes by his wit.
The clergy thrive, and the litigious bar;
Dull heroes fatten with the spoils of war:
All southern vices, Heav'n be prais'd, are here;
But wit 's a luxury you think too dear.
When you to cultivate the plant are loth,
'T is a shrewd sign 't was never of your growth;
And wit in northern climates will not blow,
Except, like orange trees, 't is hous'd from snow.
There needs no care to put a playhouse down,
'T is the most desart place of all the town:

We and our neighbours, to speak proudly, are,
Like monarchs, ruin'd with expensive war;
While, like wise English, unconcern'd you sit,
And see us play the tragedy of wit.

EPILOGUE

A pretty task! and so I told the fool,
Who needs would undertake to please by rule:
He thought that, if his characters were good,
The scenes entire, and freed from noise and blood,
The action great, yet circumscrib'd by time,
The words not forc'd, but sliding into rhyme,
The passions rais'd and calm'd by just degrees,
As tides are swell'd, and then retire to seas;
He thought, in hitting these, his bus'ness done,
Tho' he, perhaps, has fail'd in ev'ry one:
But, after all, a poet must confess,
His art's like physic, but a happy guess.
Your pleasure on your fancy must depend:
The lady's pleas'd, just as she likes her friend.
No song! no dance! no show! he fears you'll say
You love all naked beauties but a play.

SONG *from* THE SPANISH FRIAR

I   Farewell, ungrateful traitor!
      Farewell, my perjur'd swain!
    Let never injur'd creature
      Believe a man again.
    The pleasure of possessing
    Surpasses all expressing,
    But 't is too short a blessing,
      And love too long a pain.

II   'T is easy to deceive us,
      In pity of your pain;
    But when we love, you leave us
      To rail at you in vain.

Before we have descried it,
There is no bliss beside it;
But she that once has tried it
    Will never love again.

III The passion you pretended,
        Was only to obtain;
    But when the charm is ended,
        The charmer you disdain.
    Your love by ours we measure,
    Till we have lost our treasure;
    But dying is a pleasure,
        When living is a pain.

EPILOGUE *to* MITHRIDATES
Spoken by Mr. Goodman

Pox on this playhouse; 't is an old tir'd jade!
'T will do no longer; we must force a trade.
What if we all turn witness of the Plot?
That 's overstock'd; there 's nothing to be got.
Shall we take orders? That will parts require,
And colleges give no degrees for hire.
Would Salamanca was a little nigher!
Will nothing do? Oh, now 't is found, I hope!
Have not you seen the dancing of the rope?
When Andrew's wit was clean run off the score
And Jacob's cap'ring tricks could do no more,
A damsel does to the ladder's top advance
And with two heavy buckets drags a dance;
The yawning crown perch'd up to see the sight
And slaver'd at the mouth for vast delight.
Oh, friends, there 's nothing to enchant the mind,
Nothing like that sweet sex to draw mankind:
The founder'd horse that switching will not stir,
Trots to the mare afore without a spur.
Faith, I 'll go scour the scene room and engage
Some toy within to save the falling stage.

                                    [*Exit.*

  Who have we here again? what nymph 's i'th' stocks?
  Your most obedient servant, sweet Madam Cox.
  You 'd best be coy and blush for a pretense:
  For shame, say something in your own defense!
Mrs. Cox. What shall I say? I have been hence so long
  I 've e'en almost forget my mother tongue.
  If I can act I wish I were ten fathom
  Beneath—
Mr. Goodman. Oh, Lord! Pray you, no swearing madam!
Mrs. Cox. Why, sir, if I had sworn to save the nation
  I could find out some mental reservation.
  Well, in plain terms, gallants, without a sham,
  Will you be pleas'd to take me as I am:
  Quite out of countenance, with a downcast look,
  Just like a truant that returns to book.
  Yet I 'm not old; but if I were, this place
  Ne'er wanted art to piece a ruin'd face.
  When graybeards govern'd I forsook the stage;
  You know 't is piteous work to act with age.
  Tho' there 's no sex amongst these beardless boys,
  There 's what we women love: that 's mirth and noise.
  These young beginners may grow up in time,
  And the devil 's in 't if I am past my prime.

from ABSALOM AND ACHITOPHEL, PART I [lines 1–227]

  In pious times, ere priestcraft did begin,
  Before polygamy was made a sin;
  When man on many multiplied his kind,
  Ere one to one was cursedly confin'd;
  When nature prompted, and no law denied
  Promiscuous use of concubine and bride;
  Then Israel's monarch after Heaven's own heart,
  His vigorous warmth did variously impart
  To wives and slaves; and, wide as his command,
  Scatter'd his Maker's image thro' the land.
  Michal, of royal blood, the crown did wear;
  A soil ungrateful to the tiller's care:

Not so the rest; for several mothers bore
To godlike David several sons before.
But since like slaves his bed they did ascend,
No true succession could their seed attend.
Of all this numerous progeny was none
So beautiful, so brave, as Absalon:
Whether, inspir'd by some diviner lust,
His father got him with a greater gust;
Or that his conscious destiny made way,
By manly beauty, to imperial sway.
Early in foreign fields he won renown,
With kings and states allied to Israel's crown:
In peace the thoughts of war he could remove,
And seem'd as he were only born for love.
Whate'er he did, was done with so much ease,
In him alone 't was natural to please:
His motions all accompanied with grace;
And paradise was open'd in his face.
With secret joy indulgent David view'd
His youthful image in his son renew'd:
To all his wishes nothing he denied;
And made the charming Annabel his bride.
What faults he had, (for who from faults is free?)
His father could not, or he would not see.
Some warm excesses which the law forbore,
Were construed youth that purg'd by boiling o'er,
And Amnon's murther, by a specious name,
Was call'd a just revenge for injur'd fame.
Thus prais'd and lov'd the noble youth remain'd,
While David, undisturb'd, in Sion reign'd.
But life can never be sincerely blest;
Heav'n punishes the bad, and proves the best.
The Jews, a headstrong, moody, murm'ring race,
As ever tried th' extent and stretch of grace;
God's pamper'd people, whom, debauch'd with ease,
No king could govern, nor no God could please;
(Gods they had tried of every shape and size,
That god-smiths could produce, or priests devise:)
These Adam-wits, too fortunately free,

Began to dream they wanted liberty;
And when no rule, no precedent was found,
Of men by laws less circumscrib'd and bound;
They led their wild desires to woods and caves,
And thought that all but savages were slaves.
They who, when Saul was dead, without a blow,
Made foolish Ishbosheth the crown forego;
Who banish'd David did from Hebron bring,
And with a general shout proclaim'd him king:
Those very Jews, who, at their very best,
Their humour more than loyalty express'd,
Now wonder'd why so long they had obey'd
An idol monarch, which their hands had made;
Thought they might ruin him they could create,
Or melt him to that golden calf, a State.
But these were random bolts; no form'd design,
Nor interest made the factious crowd to join:
The sober part of Israel, free from stain,
Well knew the value of a peaceful reign;
And, looking backward with a wise affright,
Saw seams of wounds, dishonest to the sight:
In contemplation of whose ugly scars
They curs'd the memory of civil wars.
The moderate sort of men, thus qualified,
Inclin'd the balance to the better side;
And David's mildness manag'd it so well,
The bad found no occasion to rebel.
But when to sin our bias'd nature leans,
The careful Devil is still at hand with means;
And providently pimps for ill desires.
The Good Old Cause reviv'd, a plot requires:
Plots, true or false, are necessary things,
To raise up commonwealths, and ruin kings.
    Th' inhabitants of old Jerusalem
Were Jebusites; the town so call'd from them;
And theirs the native right ——
But when the chosen people grew more strong,
The rightful cause at length became the wrong;
And every loss the men of Jebus bore,

They still were thought God's enemies the more.
Thus worn and weaken'd, well or ill content,
Submit they must to David's government:
Impoverish'd and depriv'd of all command,
Their taxes doubled as they lost their land;
And, what was harder yet to flesh and blood,
Their gods disgrac'd, and burnt like common wood.
This set the heathen priesthood in a flame;
For priests of all religions are the same:
Of whatsoe'er descent their godhead be,
Stock, stone, or other homely pedigree,
In his defense his servants are as bold,
As if he had been born of beaten gold.
The Jewish rabbins, tho' their enemies,
In this conclude them honest men and wise:
For 't was their duty, all the learned think,
T' espouse his cause, by whom they eat and drink.
From hence began that Plot, the nation's curse,
Bad in itself, but represented worse;
Rais'd in extremes, and in extremes decried;
With oaths affirm'd, with dying vows denied;
Not weigh'd or winnow'd by the multitude;
But swallow'd in the mass, unchew'd and crude.
Some truth there was, but dash'd and brew'd with lies,
To please the fools, and puzzle all the wise.
Succeeding times did equal folly call,
Believing nothing, or believing all.
Th' Egyptian rites the Jebusites embrac'd;
Where gods were recommended by their taste.
Such sav'ry deities must needs be good,
As serv'd at once for worship and for food.
By force they could not introduce these gods,
For ten to one in former days was odds;
So fraud was us'd (the sacrificer's trade):
Fools are more hard to conquer than persuade.
Their busy teachers mingled with the Jews,
And rak'd for converts even the court and stews:
Which Hebrew priests the more unkindly took,
Because the fleece accompanies the flock.

Some thought they God's anointed meant to slay
By guns, invented since full many a day:
Our author swears it not; but who can know
How far the Devil and the Jebusites may go?
This Plot, which fail'd for want of common sense,
Had yet a deep and dangerous consequence:
For, as when raging fevers boil the blood,
The standing lake soon floats into a flood,
And ev'ry hostile humour, which before
Slept quiet in its channels, bubbles o'er;
So several factions from this first ferment
Work up to foam, and threat the government.
Some by their friends, more by themselves thought wise,
Oppos'd the pow'r to which they could not rise.
Some had in courts been great, and thrown from thence,
Like fiends were harden'd in impenitence.
Some, by their monarch's fatal mercy grown
From pardon'd rebels kinsmen to the throne,
Were rais'd in pow'r and public office high;
Strong bands, if bands ungrateful men could tie.
    Of these the false Achitophel was first;
A name to all succeeding ages curst:
For close designs and crooked counsels fit;
Sagacious, bold, and turbulent of wit;
Restless, unfix'd in principles and place;
In pow'r unpleas'd impatient of disgrace:
A fiery soul, which, working out its way,
Fretted the pigmy body to decay,
And o'er-inform'd the tenement of clay.
A daring pilot in extremity;
Pleas'd with the danger, when the waves went high,
He sought the storms; but, for a calm unfit,
Would steer too nigh the sands, to boast his wit.
Great wits are sure to madness near allied,
And thin partitions do their bounds divide;
Else why should he with wealth and honour blest,
Refuse his age the needful hours of rest?
Punish a body which he could not please;
Bankrupt of life, yet prodigal of ease?

And all to leave what with his toil he won,
To that unfeather'd two-legg'd thing, a son;
Got, while his soul did huddled notions try;
And born a shapeless lump, like anarchy.
In friendship false, implacable in hate;
Resolv'd to ruin or to rule the State.
To compass this the triple bond he broke;
The pillars of the public safety shook;
And fitted Israel for a foreign yoke:
Then seiz'd with fear, yet still affecting fame,
Usurp'd a patriot's all-atoning name.
So easy still it proves in factious times,
With public zeal to cancel private crimes.
How safe is treason, and how sacred ill,
Where none can sin against the people's will!
Where crowds can wink, and so offense be known,
Since in another's guilt they find their own!
Yet fame deserv'd no enemy can grudge;
The statesman we abhor, but praise the judge.
In Israel's courts ne'er sat an Abbethdin
With more discerning eyes, or hands more clean;
Unbrib'd, unsought, the wretched to redress;
Swift of dispatch, and easy of access.
O, had he been content to serve the crown,
With virtues only proper to the gown;
Or had the rankness of the soil been freed
From cockle, that oppress'd the noble seed;
David for him his tuneful harp had strung,
And Heav'n had wanted one immortal song.
But wild Ambition loves to slide, not stand,
And Fortune's ice prefers to Virtue's land.
Achitophel, grown weary to possess
A lawful fame, and lazy happiness,
Disdain'd the golden fruit to gather free,
And lent the crowd his arm to shake the tree.
Now, manifest of crimes contriv'd long since,
He stood at bold defiance with his prince;
Held up the buckler of the people's cause
Against the crown, and skulk'd behind the laws.

The wish'd occasion of the Plot he takes;
Some circumstances finds, but more he makes.
By buzzing emissaries fills the ears
Of list'ning crowds with jealousies and fears
Of arbitrary counsels brought to light,
And proves the king himself a Jebusite.
Weak arguments! which yet he knew full well
Were strong with people easy to rebel.
For, govern'd by the moon, the giddy Jews
Tread the same track when she the prime renews;
And once in twenty years, their scribes record,
By natural instinct they change their lord.
Architophel still wants a chief, and none
Was found so fit as warlike Absalon:
Not that he wish'd his greatness to create,
(For politicians neither love nor hate,)
But, for he knew his title not allow'd,
Would keep him still depending on the crowd:
That kingly pow'r, thus ebbing out, might be
Drawn to the dregs of a democracy.

MAC FLECKNOE
Or, a Satire upon the True-blue-protestant Poet T. S.

All human things are subject to decay,
And when fate summons, monarchs must obey.
This Flecknoe found, who, like Augustus, young
Was call'd to empire, and had govern'd long;
In prose and verse, was own'd, without dispute,
Thro' all the realms of *Nonsense*, absolute.
This aged prince, now flourishing in peace,
And blest with issue of a large increase;
Worn out with business, did at length debate
To settle the succession of the State;
And, pond'ring which of all his sons was fit
To reign, and wage immortal war with wit,
Cried: "'T is resolv'd; for nature pleads, that he
Should only rule, who most resembles me.

C

Sh— alone my perfect image bears,
Mature in dulness from his tender years:
Sh— alone, of all my sons, is he
Who stands confirm'd in full stupidity.
The rest to some faint meaning make pretense,
But Sh— never deviates into sense.
Some beams of wit on other souls may fall,
Strike thro', and make a lucid interval;
But Sh—'s genuine night admits no ray,
His rising fogs prevail upon the day.
Besides, his goodly fabric fills the eye,
And seems design'd for thoughtless majesty;
Thoughtless as monarch oaks that shade the plain,
And, spread in solemn state, supinely reign.
Heywood and Shirley were but types of thee,
Thou last great prophet of tautology.
Even I, a dunce of more renown than they,
Was sent before but to prepare thy way;
And, coarsely clad in Norwich drugget, came
To teach the nations in thy greater name.
My warbling lute, the lute I whilom strung,
When to King John of Portugal I sung,
Was but the prelude to that glorious day,
When thou on silver Thames didst cut thy way,
With well-tim'd oars before the royal barge,
Swell'd with the pride of thy celestial charge;
And big with hymn, commander of a host,
The like was ne'er in Epsom blankets toss'd.
Methinks I see the new Arion sail,
The lute still trembling underneath thy nail.
At thy well-sharpen'd thumb from shore to shore
The treble squeaks for fear, the basses roar;
Echoes from Pissing Alley Sh— call,
And Sh— they resound from Aston Hall.
About thy boat the little fishes throng,
As at the morning toast that floats along.
Sometimes, as prince of thy harmonious band,
Thou wield'st thy papers in thy threshing hand.
St. André's feet ne'er kept more equal time,

Not ev'n the feet of thy own *Psyche's* rhyme;
Tho' they in number as in sense excel:
So just, so like tautology, they fell,
That, pale with envy, Singleton forswore
The lute and sword, which he in triumph bore,
And vow'd he ne'er would act Villerius more."
Here stopp'd the good old sire, and wept for joy
In silent raptures of the hopeful boy.
All arguments, but most his plays, persuade,
That for anointed dulness he was made.

  Close to the walls which fair Augusta bind,
(The fair Augusta much to fears inclin'd,)
An ancient fabric rais'd t' inform the sight,
There stood of yore, and Barbican it hight:
A watchtower once; but now, so fate ordains,
Of all the pile an empty name remains.
From its old ruins brothel-houses rise,
Scenes of lewd loves, and of polluted joys,
Where their vast courts the mother-strumpets keep,
And, undisturb'd by watch, in silence sleep.
Near these a Nursery erects its head,
Where queens are form'd, and future heroes bred;
Where unfledg'd actors learn to laugh and cry,
Where infant punks their tender voices try,
And little Maximins the gods defy.
Great Fletcher never treads in buskins here,
Nor greater Jonson dares in socks appear;
But gentle Simkin just reception finds
Amidst this monument of vanish'd minds:
Pure clinches the suburbian Muse affords,
And Panton waging harmless war with words.
Here Flecknoe, as a place to fame well known,
Ambitiously design'd his Sh—'s throne;
For ancient Dekker prophesied long since,
That in this pile should reign a mighty prince,
Born for a scourge of wit, and flail of sense;
To whom true dulness should some *Psyches* owe,
But worlds of *Misers* from his pen should flow;
Humorists and *Hypocrites* it should produce.

Whole Raymond families, and tribes of Bruce.
  Now Empress Fame had publish'd the renown
Of Sh—'s coronation thro' the town.
Rous'd by report of Fame, the nations meet,
From near Bunhill, and distant Watling Street.
No Persian carpets spread th' imperial way,
But scatter'd limbs of mangled poets lay;
From dusty shops neglected authors come,
Martyrs of pies, and relics of the bum.
Much Heywood, Shirley, Ogleby there lay,
But loads of Sh— almost chok'd the way.
Bilk'd stationers for yeomen stood prepar'd,
And Herringman was captain of the guard.
The hoary prince in majesty appear'd,
High on a throne of his own labours rear'd.
At his right hand our young Ascanius sate,
Rome's other hope, and pillar of the State.
His brows thick fogs, instead of glories, grace,
And lambent dulness play'd around his face.
As Hannibal did to the altars come,
Sworn by his sire a mortal foe to Rome;
So Sh— swore, nor should his vow be vain,
That he till death true dulness would maintain;
And, in his father's right, and realm's defense,
Ne'er to have peace with wit, nor truce with sense.
The king himself the sacred unction made,
As king by office, and as priest by trade.
In his sinister hand, instead of ball,
He plac'd a mighty mug of potent ale;
Love's Kingdom to his right he did convey,
At once his sceptre, and his rule of sway;
Whose righteous lore the prince had practic'd young,
And from whose loins recorded *Psyche* sprung.
His temples, last, with poppies were o'er-spread,
That nodding seem'd to consecrate his head.
Just at that point of time, if fame not lie,
On his left hand twelve reverend owls did fly.
So Romulus, 't is sung, by Tiber's brook,
Presage of sway from twice six vultures took.

Th' admiring throng loud acclamations make,
And omens of his future empire take.
The sire then shook the honours of his head,
And from his brows damps of oblivion shed
Full on the filial dulness: long he stood,
Repelling from his breast the raging god;
At length burst out in this prophetic mood:
    "Heavens bless my son, from Ireland let him reign
To far Barbadoes on the western main;
Of his dominion may no end be known,
And greater than his father's be his throne;
Beyond *Love's Kingdom* let him stretch his pen!"
He paus'd, and all the people cried, "Amen."
Then thus continued he: "My son, advance
Still in new impudence, new ignorance.
Success let others teach, learn thou from me
Pangs without birth, and fruitless industry.
Let *Virtuosos* in five years be writ;
Yet not one thought accuse thy toil of wit.
Let gentle George in triumph tread the stage,
Make Dorimant betray, and Loveit rage;
Let Cully, Cockwood, Fopling, charm the pit,
And in their folly shew the writer's wit.
Yet still thy fools shall stand in thy defense,
And justify their author's want of sense.
Let 'em be all by thy own model made
Of dulness, and desire no foreign aid;
That they to future ages may be known,
Not copies drawn, but issue of thy own.
Nay, let thy men of wit too be the same,
All full of thee, and differing but in name.
But let no alien S—dl—y interpose,
To lard with wit thy hungry *Epsom* prose.
And when false flowers of rhetoric thou wouldst cull,
Trust nature, do not labour to be dull;
But write thy best, and top; and, in each line,
Sir Formal's oratory will be thine:
Sir Formal, tho' unsought, attends thy quill,
And does thy northern dedications fill.

Nor let false friends seduce thy mind to fame,
By arrogating Jonson's hostile name.
Let father Flecknoe fire thy mind with praise,
And uncle Ogleby thy envy raise.
Thou art my blood, where Jonson has no part:
What share have we in nature, or in art?
Where did his wit on learning fix a brand,
And rail at arts he did not understand?
Where made he love in Prince Nicander's vein,
Or swept the dust in *Psyche's* humble strain?
Where sold he bargains, 'whip-stitch, kiss my arse,'
Promis'd a play and dwindled to a farce?
When did his Muse from Fletcher scenes purloin,
As thou whole Eth'rege dost transfuse to thine?
But so transfus'd, as oil on water's flow,
His always floats above, thine sinks below.
This is thy province, this thy wondrous way,
New humors to invent for each new play:
This is that boasted bias of thy mind,
By which one way, to dulness, 't is inclin'd;
Which makes thy writings lean on one side still,
And, in all changes, that way bends thy will.
Nor let thy mountain-belly make pretense
Of likeness; thine's a tympany of sense.
A tun of man in thy large bulk is writ,
But sure thou 'rt but a kilderkin of wit.
Like mine, thy gentle numbers feebly creep;
Thy tragic Muse gives smiles, thy comic sleep.
With whate'er gall thou sett'st thyself to write,
Thy inoffensive satires never bite.
In thy felonious heart tho' venom lies,
It does but touch thy Irish pen, and dies.
Thy genius calls thee not to purchase fame
In keen iambics, but mild anagram.
Leave writing plays, and choose for thy command
Some peaceful province in acrostic land.
There thou may'st wings display and altars raise,
And torture one poor word ten thousand ways.
Or, if thou wouldst thy diff'rent talents suit,

Set thy own songs, and sing them to thy lute."
    He said: but his last words were scarcely heard;
For Bruce and Longvil had a trap prepar'd,
And down they sent the yet declaiming bard.
Sinking he left his drugget robe behind,
Borne upwards by a subterranean wind.
The mantle fell to the young prophet's part,
With double portion of his father's art.

from ABSALOM AND ACHITOPHEL, PART II [lines 400–509]

    Levi, thou art a load, I'll lay thee down,
And shew rebellion bare, without a gown;
Poor slaves in meter, dull and addle-pated,
Who rhyme below ev'n David's psalms translated;
Some in my speedy pace I must outrun,
As lame Mephibosheth the wizard's son;
To make quick way I'll leap o'er heavy blocks,
Shun rotten Uzza, as I would the pox
And hasten Og and Doeg to rehearse,
Two fools that crutch their feeble sense on verse;
Who, by my Muse, to all succeeding times
Shall live, in spite of their own dogg'rel rhymes.
    Doeg, tho' without knowing how or why,
Made still a blund'ring kind of melody;
Spurr'd boldly on, and dash'd thro' thick and thin,
Thro' sense and nonsense, never out nor in;
Free from all meaning, whether good or bad,
And, in one word, heroically mad:
He was too warm on picking-work to dwell,
But fagoted his notions as they fell,
And if they rhym'd and rattled, all was well.
Spiteful he is not, tho' he wrote a satire,
For still there goes some *thinking* to ill-nature:
He needs no more than birds and beasts to think;
All his occasions are to eat and drink.
If he call rogue and rascal from a garret,
He means you no more mischief than a parrot;

The words for friend and foe alike were made,
To fetter 'em in verse is all his trade.
For almonds he 'll cry whore to his own mother;
And call young Absalom King David's brother.
Let him be gallows-free by my consent,
And nothing suffer, since he nothing meant;
Hanging supposes human soul and reason,
This animal 's below committing treason.
Shall he be hang'd who never could rebel?
That 's a preferment for Achitophel.
The woman that committed buggary,
Was rightly sentenc'd by the law to die;
But 't was hard fate that to the gallows led
The dog that never heard the statute read.
Railing in other men may be a crime,
But ought to pass for mere instinct in him:
Instinct he follows, and no farther knows,
For to write verse with him is to *transprose*.
'T were pity treason at his door to lay,
Who *makes heaven's gate a lock to its own key:*
Let him rail on, let his invective Muse
Have four and twenty letters to abuse,
Which if he jumbles to one line of sense,
Indict him of a capital offense.
In fireworks give him leave to vent his spite,
Those are the only serpents he can write;
The height of his ambition is, we know,
But to be master of a puppet show:
On that one stage his works may yet appear,
And a month's harvest keeps him all the year.
 Now stop your noses, readers, all and some,
For here 's a tun of midnight work to come,
Og, from a treason-tavern rolling home.
Round as a globe, and liquor'd ev'ry chink,
Goodly and great he sails behind his link.
With all this bulk there 's nothing lost in Og,
For ev'ry inch that is not fool is rogue:
A monstrous mass of foul corrupted matter,
As all the devils had spew'd to make the batter.

When wine has given him courage to blaspheme,
He curses God, but God before curs'd him;
And if man could have reason, none has more,
That made his paunch so rich, and him so poor.
With wealth he was not trusted, for Heav'n knew
What 't was of old to pamper up a Jew;
To what would he on quail and pheasant swell,
That ev'n on tripe and carrion could rebel?
But tho' Heav'n made him poor, (with rev'rence speaking,)
He never was a poet of God's making.
The midwife laid her hand on his thick skull,
With this prophetic blessing: *Be thou dull*;
Drink, swear, and roar, forbear no lewd delight
Fit for thy bulk, do anything but write:
Thou art of lasting make, like thoughtless men,
A strong nativity—but for the pen;
Eat opium, mingle arsenic in thy drink,
Still thou mayst live, avoiding pen and ink.
I see, I see, 't is counsel given in vain,
For treason botch'd in rhyme will be thy bane;
Rhyme is the rock on which thou art to wreck,
'T is fatal to thy fame and to thy neck:
Why should thy meter good King David blast?
A psalm of his will surely be thy last.
Dar'st thou presume in verse to meet thy foes,
Thou whom the penny pamphlet foil'd in prose?
Doeg, whom God for mankind's mirth has made.
O'ertops thy talent in thy very trade;
Doeg to thee, thy paintings are so coarse,
A poet is, tho' he 's the poets' horse.
A double noose thou on thy neck dost pull,
For writing treason, and for writing dull;
To die for faction is a common evil,
But to be hang'd for nonsense is the devil:
Hadst thou the glories of thy king express'd,
Thy praises had been satire at the best;
But thou in clumsy verse, unlick'd, unpointed,
Hast shamefully defied the Lord's anointed:
I will not rake the dunghill of thy crimes,

For who would read thy life that reads thy rhymes?
But of King David's foes, be this the doom,
May all be like the young man Absalom;
And for my foes may this their blessing be,
To talk like Doeg, and to write like thee.

from RELIGIO LAICI [lines 1–183]

Dim as the borrow'd beams of moon and stars
To lonely, weary, wand'ring travellers,
Is Reason to the soul; and, as on high
Those rolling fires discover but the sky,
Not light us here, so Reason's glimmering ray
Was lent, not to assure our doubtful way,
But guide us upward to a better day.
And as those nightly tapers disappear,
When day's bright lord ascends our hemisphere;
So pale grows Reason at Religion's sight;
So dies, and so dissolves in supernatural light.
Some few, whose lamp shone brighter, have been led
From cause to cause, to nature's secret head;
And found that one first principle must be:
But what, or who, that UNIVERSAL HE;
Whether some soul incompassing this ball,
Unmade, unmov'd; yet making, moving all;
Or various atoms' interfering dance
Leapt into form, (the noble work of chance;)
Or this great all was from eternity;
Not ev'n the Stagirite himself could see,
And Epicurus guess'd as well as he:
As blindly grop'd they for a future state;
As rashly judg'd of providence and fate:

Opinions of the several sects of philosophers concerning the *Summum Bonum.*

But least of all could their endeavours find
What most concern'd the good of humankind;
For happiness was never to be found,
But vanish'd from 'em like enchanted ground.

One thought content the good to be enjoy'd;
This every little accident destroy'd:
The wiser madmen did for virtue toil,
A thorny, or at best a barren soil;
In pleasure some their glutton souls would steep,
But found their line too short, the well too deep,
And leaky vessels which no bliss could keep.
Thus anxious thoughts in endless circles roll,
Without a centre where to fix the soul;
In this wild maze their vain endeavours end:
How can the less the greater comprehend?
Or finite reason reach Infinity?
For what could fathom GOD were more than He.

System of Deism.

The Deist thinks he stands on firmer ground;
Cries: "$E\H{\upsilon}\rho\epsilon\kappa\alpha$, the mighty secret 's found:
God is that spring of good; supreme and best;
We, made to serve, and in that service blest."
If so, some rules of worship must be given,
Distributed alike to all by Heaven:
Else God were partial, and to some denied
The means his justice should for all provide.
This general worship is to PRAISE and PRAY,
One part to borrow blessings, one to pay;
And when frail nature slides into offense,
The sacrifice for crimes is penitence.
Yet, since th' effects of providence, we find,
Are variously dispens'd to humankind;
That vice triumphs, and virtue suffers here,
(A brand that sovereign justice cannot bear;)
Our reason prompts us to a future state,
The last appeal from fortune and from fate:
Where God's all-righteous ways will be declar'd,
The bad meet punishment, the good reward.
Thus man by his own strength to heaven would soar,

Of reveal'd Religion.

And would not be oblig'd to God for more.
Vain, wretched creature, how art thou misled

To think thy wit these godlike notions bred!
These truths are not the product of thy mind,
But dropp'd from heaven, and of a nobler kind.
Reveal'd Religion first inform'd thy sight,
And Reason saw not, till Faith sprung the light.
Hence all thy natural worship takes the source:
'T is revelation what thou think'st discourse.
Else, how com'st thou to see these truths so clear,
Which so obscure to heathens did appear?
Not Plato these, not Aristotle found;
Nor he whose wisdom oracles renown'd.

Socrates.

Hast thou a wit so deep, or so sublime,
Or canst thou lower dive, or higher climb?
Canst thou, by Reason, more of Godhead know
Than Plutarch, Seneca, or Cicero?
Those giant wits, in happier ages born,
(When arms and arts did Greece and Rome adorn,)
Knew no such system; no such piles could raise
Of natural worship, built on pray'r and praise,
To One Sole God:
Nor did remorse to expiate sin prescribe,
But slew their fellow creatures for a bribe:
The guiltless victim groan'd for their offense,
And cruelty and blood was penitence.
If sheep and oxen could atone for men,
Ah! at how cheap a rate the rich might sin!
And great oppressors might Heaven's wrath beguile,
By offering his own creatures for a spoil!
    Dar'st thou, poor worm, offend Infinity?
And must the terms of peace be given by thee?
Then thou art Justice in the last appeal:
Thy easy God instructs thee to rebel;
And, like a king remote, and weak, must take
What satisfaction thou art pleas'd to make.
    But if there be a pow'r too just and strong
To wink at crimes, and bear unpunish'd wrong;
Look humbly upward, see his will disclose

The forfeit first, and then the fine impose:
A mulct thy poverty could never pay,
Had not eternal wisdom found the way,
And with celestial wealth supplied thy store:
His justice makes the fine, his mercy quits the score.
See God descending in thy human frame;
Th' offended suff'ring in th' offender's name;
All thy misdeeds to him imputed see,
And all his righteousness devolv'd on thee.

   For granting we have sinn'd, and that th' offense
Of man is made against Omnipotence,
Some price that bears proportion must be paid,
And infinite with infinite be weigh'd.
See then the Deist lost: remorse for vice,
Not paid; or paid, inadequate in price:
What farther means can Reason now direct,
Or what relief from human wit expect?
That shews us sick; and sadly are we sure
Still to be sick, till Heav'n reveal the cure:
If then Heav'n's will must needs be understood,
(Which must, if we want cure, and Heaven be good,)
Let all records of will reveal'd be shown;
With Scripture all in equal balance thrown,
And our one sacred book will be that one.

   Proof needs not here, for whether we compare
That impious, idle, superstitious ware
Of rites, lustrations, offerings, (which before,
In various ages, various countries bore,)
With Christian faith and virtues, we shall find
None answ'ring the great ends of humankind,
But this one rule of life, that shews us best
How God may be appeas'd, and mortals blest.
Whether from length of time its worth we draw,
The world is scarce more ancient than the law:
Heav'n's early care prescrib'd for every age;
First, in the soul, and after, in the page.
Or, whether more abstractedly we look,
Or on the writers, or the written book,
Whence, but from heav'n, could men unskill'd in arts,

In several ages born, in several parts,
Weave such agreeing truths? or how, or why,
Should all conspire to cheat us with a lie?
Unask'd their pains, ungrateful their advice,
Starving their gain, and martyrdom their price.

If on the book itself we cast our view,
Concurrent heathens prove the story true;
The doctrine, miracles; which must convince,
For Heav'n in them appeals to human sense:
And tho' they prove not, they confirm the cause,
When what is taught agrees with nature's laws.

Then for the style; majestic and divine,
It speaks no less than God in every line:
Commanding words; whose force is still the same
As the first fiat that produc'd our frame.
All faiths beside or did by arms ascend,
Or sense indulg'd has made mankind their friend:
This only doctrine does our lusts oppose,
Unfed by nature's soil, in which it grows;
Cross to our interests, curbing sense and sin;
Oppress'd without, and undermin'd within,
It thrives thro' pain; its own tormentors tires;
And with a stubborn patience still aspires.
To what can Reason such effects assign,
Transcending nature, but to laws divine?
Which in that sacred volume are contain'd;
Sufficient, clear, and for that use ordain'd.

But stay: the Deist here will urge anew,

Objection of the Deist.

No supernatural worship can be true;
Because a general law is that alone
Which must to all, and everywhere, be known:
A style so large as not this book can claim,
Nor aught that bears reveal'd Religion's name.
'T is said the sound of a Messiah's birth
Is gone thro' all the habitable earth;
But still that text must be confin'd alone
To what was then inhabited, and known:

And what provision could from thence accrue
To Indian souls, and worlds discover'd new?
In other parts it helps, that, ages past,
The Scriptures there were known, and were imbrac'd,
Till Sin spread once again the shades of night:
What's that to these who never saw the light?

PROLOGUE TO THE KING AND QUEEN AT THE
OPENING OF THEIR THEATRE
Spoken by Mr. Betterton

Since faction ebbs, and rogues grow out of fashion,
Their penny scribes take care t' inform the nation,
How well men thrive in this or that plantation:

How Pennsylvania's air agrees with Quakers,
And Carolina's with Associators:
Both e'en too good for madmen and for traitors.

Truth is, our land with saints is so run o'er,
And every age produces such a store,
That now there 's need of two New Englands more.

"What's this," you 'll say, "to us and our vocation?"
Only thus much, that we have left our station,
And made this theatre our new plantation.

The factious natives never could agree;
But aiming, as they call'd it, to be free,
Those playhouse Whigs set up for property.

Some say they no obedience paid of late,
But would new fears and jealousies create,
Till topsy-turvy they had turn'd the State.

Plain sense, without the talent of foretelling,
Might guess 't would end in downright knocks and quelling;
For seldom comes there better of rebelling.

When men will, needlessly, their freedom barter
For lawless pow'r, sometimes they catch a Tartar;
(There's a damn'd word that rhymes to this, call'd Charter.)

But, since the victory with us remains,
You shall be call'd to twelve in all our gains;
(If you 'll not think us saucy for our pains.)

Old men shall have good old plays to delight 'em;
And you, fair ladies and gallants, that slight 'em,
We 'll treat with good new plays; if our new wits can write
    'em.

We 'll take no blund'ring verse, no fustian tumour,
No dribbling love, from this or that presumer;
No dull fat fool shamm'd on the stage for humour.

For, faith, some of 'em such vile stuff have made,
As none but fools or fairies ever play'd;
But 't was, as shopmen say, to force a trade.

We 've giv'n you tragedies, all sense defying,
And singing men, in woful metre dying:
This 't is when heavy lubbers will be flying.

All these disasters we well hope to weather;
We bring you none of our old lumber hether:
Whig poets and Whig sheriffs may hang together.

PROLOGUE TO THE UNIVERSITY OF OXFORD
Spoken by Mr. Hart, at the acting of The Silent Woman

What Greece, when learning flourish'd, only knew,
Athenian judges, you this day renew.
Here too are annual rites to Pallas done,
And here poetic prizes lost or won.
Methinks I see you, crown'd with olives, sit,
And strike a sacred horror from the pit.
A day of doom is this of your decree,
Where even the best are but by mercy free:

A day, which none but Jonson durst have wish'd to see.
Here they, who long have known the useful stage,
Come to be taught themselves to teach the age.
As your commissioners our poets go,
To cultivate the virtue which you sow;
In your Lycæum first themselves refin'd,
And delegated thence to humankind.
But as embassadors, when long from home,
For new instructions to their princes come;
So poets, who your precepts have forgot,
Return, and beg they may be better taught:
Follies and faults elsewhere by them are shown,
But by your manners they correct their own.
Th' illiterate writer, empiric-like, applies
To minds diseas'd, unsafe, chance remedies:
The learn'd in schools, where knowledge first began,
Studies with care th' anatomy of man;
Sees virtue, vice, and passions in their cause,
And fame from science, not from fortune, draws.
So poetry, which is in Oxford made
An art, in London only is a trade.
There haughty dunces, whose unlearned pen
Could ne'er spell grammar, would be reading men.
Such build their poems the Lucretian way;
So many huddled atoms make a play;
And if they hit in order by some chance,
They call that nature, which is ignorance.
To such a fame let mere town-wits aspire,
And their gay nonsense their own cits admire.
Our poet, could he find forgiveness here,
Would wish it rather than a *plaudit* there.
He owns no crown from those Prætorian bands,
But knows *that* right is in this senate's hands.
Not impudent enough to hope your praise,
Low at the Muses' feet his wreath he lays,
And, where he took it up, resigns his bays.
Kings make their poets whom themselves think fit,
But 't is your suffrage makes authentic wit.

Oft has our poet wish'd, this happy seat
Might prove his fading Muse's last retreat:
I wonder'd at his wish, but now I find
He here sought quiet, and content of mind;
Which noiseful towns and courts can never know,
And only in the shades like laurels grow.
Youth, ere it sees the world, here studies rest,
And age returning thence concludes it best.
What wonder if we court that happiness
Yearly to share, which hourly you possess,
Teaching ev'n you, while the vex'd world we show,
Your peace to value more, and better know?
'T is all we can return for favours past,
Whose holy memory shall ever last,
For patronage from him whose care presides
O'er every noble art, and every science guides:
Bathurst, a name the learn'd with rev'rence know,
And scarcely more to his own Virgil owe;
Whose age enjoys but what his youth deserv'd,
To rule those Muses whom before he serv'd.
His learning, and untainted manners too,
We find, Athenians, are deriv'd to you:
Such ancient hospitality there rests
In yours, as dwelt in the first Grecian breasts,
Where kindness was religion to their guests.
Such modesty did to our sex appear,
As, had there been no laws, we need not fear,
Since each of you was our protector here.
Converse so chaste, and so strict virtue shown,
As might Apollo with the Muses own.
Till our return, we must despair to find
Judges so just, so knowing, and so kind.

Whether the fruitful Nile, or Tyrian shore,
The seeds of arts and infant science bore,
'T is sure the noble plant, translated first,
Advanc'd its head in Grecian gardens nurs'd.
The Grecians added verse; their tuneful tongue
Made nature first and nature's God their song.
Nor stopp'd translation here; for conquering Rome
With Grecian spoils brought Grecian numbers home,
Enrich'd by those Athenian Muses more
Than all the vanquish'd world could yield before;
Till barb'rous nations, and more barb'rous times,
Debas'd the majesty of verse to rhymes;
Those rude at first: a kind of hobbling prose,
That limp'd along, and tinkled in the close.
But Italy, reviving from the trance
Of Vandal, Goth, and monkish ignorance,
With pauses, cadence, and well-vowel'd words,
And all the graces a good ear affords,
Made rhyme an art, and Dante's polish'd page
Restor'd a silver, not a golden age.
Then Petrarch follow'd and in him we see
What rhyme improv'd in all its height can be:
At best a pleasing sound, and fair barbarity.
The French pursued their steps; and Britain, last,
In manly sweetness all the rest surpass'd.
The wit of Greece, the gravity of Rome,
Appear exalted in the British loom;
The Muses' empire is restor'd again,
In Charles his reign, and by Roscommon's pen.
Yet modestly he does his work survey,
And calls a finish'd poem an *Essay*;
For all the needful rules are scatter'd here;
Truth smoothly told, and pleasantly severe;
So well is art disguis'd, for nature to appear.
Nor need those rules, to give translation light:
His own example is a flame so bright,

That he who but arrives to copy well,
Unguided will advance, unknowing will excel.
Scare his own Horace could such rules ordain,
Or his own Virgil sing a nobler strain.
How much in him may rising Ireland boast,
How much in gaining him has Britain lost!
Their island in revenge has ours reclaim'd;
The more instructed we, the more we still are sham'd.
'T is well for us his generous blood did flow,
Deriv'd from British channels long ago;
That here his conquering ancestors were nurs'd,
And Ireland but translated England first:
By this reprisal we regain our right,
Else must the two contending nations fight;
A nobler quarrel for his native earth,
Than what divided Greece for Homer's birth.
To what perfection will our tongue arrive,
How will invention and translation thrive,
When authors nobly born will bear their part,
And not disdain th' inglorious praise of art!
Great generals thus, descending from command,
With their own toil provoke the soldier's hand.
How will sweet Ovid's ghost be pleas'd to hear
His fame augmented by an English peer*;
How he embellishes his Helen's loves,
Outdoes his softness, and his sense improves?
When these translate, and teach translators too,
Nor firstling kid, nor any vulgar vow
Should at Apollo's grateful altar stand:
Roscommon writes; to that auspicious hand,
Muse, feed the bull that spurns the yellow sand:
Roscommon, whom both court and camps commend,
True to his prince, and faithful to his friend;
Roscommon, first in fields of honour known,
First in the peaceful triumphs of the gown,
Who both Minervas justly makes his own.
Now let the few belov'd by Jove, and they
Whom infus'd Titan form'd of better clay,

*The Earl of Mulgrave.

On equal terms with ancient wit ingage,
Nor mighty Homer fear, nor sacred Virgil's page:
Our English palace opens wide in state,
And without stooping they may pass the gate.

TO THE MEMORY OF MR. OLDHAM

Farewell, too little, and too lately known,
Whom I began to think and call my own:
For sure our souls were near allied, and thine
Cast in the same poetic mould with mine.
One common note on either lyre did strike,
And knaves and fools we both abhorr'd alike.
To the same goal did both our studies drive;
The last set out the soonest did arrive.
Thus Nisus fell upon the slippery place,
While his young friend perform'd and won the race.
O early ripe! to thy abundant store
What could advancing age have added more?
It might (what nature never gives the young)
Have taught the numbers of thy native tongue.
But satire needs not those, and wit will shine
Thro' the harsh cadence of a rugged line:
A noble error, and but seldom made,
When poets are by too much force betray'd.
Thy generous fruits, tho' gather'd ere their prime,
Still shew'd a quickness; and maturing time
But mellows what we write to the dull sweets of rhyme.
Once more, hail and farewell; farewell, thou young,
But ah too short, Marcellus of our tongue;
Thy brows with ivy, and with laurels bound;
But fate and gloomy night encompass thee around.

from THRENODIA AUGUSTALIS [lines 78–195]

III O wondrous changes of a fatal scene,
Still varying to the last!
Heav'n, tho' its hard decree was past,
Seem'd pointing to a gracious turn again:
And death's uplifted arm arrested in its haste.

Heav'n half repented of the doom,
And almost griev'd it had foreseen,
    What by foresight it will'd eternally to come.
Mercy above did hourly plead
    For her resemblance here below,
And mild forgiveness intercede
    To stop the coming blow.
New miracles approach'd th' ethereal throne,
Such as his wondrous life had oft and lately known,
And urg'd that still they might be shown.
    On earth his pious brother pray'd and vow'd,
        Renouncing greatness at so dear a rate,
    Himself defending, what he could,
        From all the glories of his future fate.
    With him th' innumerable crowd
        Of armed prayers
Knock'd at the gates of heav'n, and knock'd aloud;
        The first, well-meaning, rude petitioners.
All for his life assail'd the throne,
All would have brib'd the skies by off'ring up their own.
So great a throng not heav'n itself could bar;
'T was almost borne by force, as in the giants' war.
The pray'rs, at least, for his reprieve were heard;
His death, like Hezekiah's, was deferr'd:
    Against the sun the shadow went;
    Five days, those five degrees, were lent
    To form our patience and prepare th' event.
The second causes took the swift command,
The med'cinal head, the ready hand,
All eager to perform their part;
All but eternal doom was conquer'd by their art:
Once more the fleeting soul came back
    T' inspire the mortal frame;
And in the body took a doubtful stand,
    Doubtful and hov'ring like expiring flame,
That mounts and falls by turns, and trembles o'er the brand.

IV The joyful short-liv'd news soon spread around,
    Took the same train, the same impetuous bound:

The drooping town in smiles again was dress'd,
Gladness in every face express'd,
Their eyes before their tongues confess'd.
Men met each other with erected look,
The steps were higher that they took,
Friends to congratulate their friends made haste,
And long-inveterate foes saluted as they pass'd:
Above the rest heroic James appear'd
Exalted more, because he more had fear'd;
His manly heart, whose noble pride
      Was still above
Dissembled hate or varnish'd love,
Its more then common transport could not hide;
But like an *eagre** rode in triumph o'er the tide.
Thus, in alternate course,
      The tyrant passions, hope and fear,
      Did in extremes appear,
And flash'd upon the soul with equal force.
Thus, at half ebb, a rolling sea
      Returns and wins upon the shore;
      The wat'ry herd, affrighted at the roar,
Rest on their fins a while, and stay,
Then backward take their wond'ring way:
The prophet wonders more than they,
      At prodigies but rarely seen before,
And cries, a *king* must fall, or kingdoms change their sway.
Such were our counter-tides at land, and so
Presaging of the fatal blow,
In their prodigious ebb and flow.
The royal soul, that like the labouring moon,
By charms of art was hurried down,
Forc'd with regret to leave her native sphere,
Came but a while on liking here:
Soon weary of the painful strife,
And made but faint essays of life:
      An evening light
      Soon shut in night;

*An eagre is a tide swelling above another tide, which I have myself observ'd
on the river Trent.

A strong distemper, and a weak relief,
Short intervals of joy, and long returns of grief.

v   The sons of art all med'cines tried,
     And every noble remedy applied;
     With emulation each essay'd
     His utmost skill, nay more, they pray'd:
     Never was losing game with better conduct play'd.
     Death never won a stake with greater toil,
     Nor e'er was fate so near a foil;
     But, like a fortress on a rock,
     Th' impregnable disease their vain attempts did mock.
     They min'd it near, they batter'd from afar
     With all the cannon of the med'cinal war;
     No gentle means could be essay'd,
     'T was beyond parley when the siege was laid.
     Th' extremest ways they first ordain,
     Prescribing such intolerable pain,
     As none but Cæsar could sustain:
     Undaunted Cæsar underwent
     The malice of their art, nor bent
     Beneath whate'er their pious rigour could invent.
     In five such days he suffer'd more
     Then any suffer'd in his reign before;
     More, infinitely more, than he
     Against the worst of rebels could decree,
     A traitor, or twice pardon'd enemy.
     Now art was tir'd without success,
     No racks could make the stubborn malady confess.
          The vain *insurancers* of life,
     And he who most perform'd and promis'd less,
          Even Short himself forsook th' unequal strife.
     Death and despair was in their looks,
     No longer they consult their memories or books;
     Like helpless friends, who view from shore
     The labouring ship, and hear the tempest roar;
          So stood they with their arms across;
     Not to assist, but to deplore
          Th' inevitable loss.

"One in herself, not rent by schism, but sound,
Entire, one solid shining diamond;

[Marks of the Catholic Church from the Nicene Creed.
Not sparkles shatter'd into sects like you:
One is the Church, and must be to be true;
One central principle of unity.
    "As undivided, so from errors free,
As one in faith, so one in sanctity.
Thus she, and none but she, th' insulting rage
Of hereties oppos'd from age to age:
Still when the giant-brood invades her throne,
She stoops from heav'n, and meets 'em halfway down,
And with paternal thunder vindicates her crówn.
But like Egyptian sorcerers you stand,
And vainly lift aloft your magic wand,
To sweep away the swarms of vermin from the land:
You could, like them, with like infernal force,
Produce the plague, but not arrest the course.
But when the boils and botches, with disgrace
And public scandal, sat upon the face,
Themselves attack'd, the *Magi* strove no more,
They saw God's finger, and their fate deplore;
Themselves they could not cure of the dishonest sore.
    "Thus one, thus pure, behold her largely spread,
Like the fair ocean from her mother-bed;
From east to west triumphantly she rides,
All shores are water'd by her wealthy tides:
The gospel-sound diffus'd from pole to pole,
Where winds can carry, and where waves can roll;
The selfsame doctrine of the sacred page
Convey'd to ev'ry clime, in ev'ry age.
    "Here let my sorrow give my satire place,
To raise new blushes on my British race;
Our sailing ships like common shores we use,
And thro' our distant colonies diffuse
The draughts of dungeons, and the stench of stews;

Whom, when their home-bred honesty is lost,
We disembogue on some far Indian coast:
Thieves, panders, palliards, sins of ev'ry sort;
Those are the manufactures we export;
And these the *missioners* our zeal has made:
For, with my country's pardon be it said,
Religion is the least of all our trade.

   "Yet some improve their traffic more than we;
For they on gain, their only god, rely;
And set a public price on piety.
Industrious of the needle and the chart,
They run full sail to their Japonian mart;
Prevention fear, and, prodigal of fame,
Sell all of Christian to the very name;
Nor leave enough of that to hide their naked shame.

   "Thus, of three marks, which in the Creed we view,
Not one of all can be applied to you:
Much less the fourth; in vain, alas, you seek
Th' ambitious title of apostolic:
Godlike descent! 't is well your blood can be
Prov'd noble in the third or fourth degree:
For all of ancient that you had before
(I mean what is not borrow'd from our store)
Was error fulminated o'er and o'er;
Old heresies condemn'd in ages past,
By care and time recover'd from the blast.

   "'T is said with ease, but never can be prov'd,
The Church her old foundations has remov'd,
And built new doctrines on unstable sands:
Judge that, ye winds and rains; you prov'd her, yet she
       stands.
Those ancient doctrines, charg'd on her for new,
Shew when, and how, and from what hands they grew.
We claim no pow'r, when heresies grow bold.
To coin new faith, but still declare the old.
How else could that obscene disease be purg'd,
When controverted texts are vainly urg'd?
To prove tradition new, there's somewhat more
Requir'd, than saying: ''T was not us'd before.'

Those monumental arms are never stirr'd,
Till schism or heresy call down Goliah's sword.
   "Thus, what you call corruptions are, in truth,
The first plantations of the gospel's youth;
Old standard faith; but cast your eyes again,
And view those errors which new sects maintain,
Or which of old disturb'd the Church's peaceful reign;
And we can point each period of the time,
When they began, and who begot the crime;
Can calculate how long th' eclipse endur'd,
Who interpos'd, what digits were obscur'd:
Of all which are already pass'd away,
We know the rise, the progress, and decay.
   "Despair at our foundations then to strike,
Till you can prove your faith apostolic;
A limpid stream drawn from the native source;
Succession lawful in a lineal course.
Prove any Church, oppos'd to this our head,
So one, so pure, so unconfin'dly spread,
Under one chief of the spiritual State,
The members all combin'd, and all subordinate.
Shew such a seamless coat, from schism so free,
In no communion join'd with heresy.
If such a one you find, let truth prevail;
Till when, your weights will in the balance fail:
A Church unprincipled kicks up the scale."

A SONG FOR ST. CECILIA'S DAY, 1687

  I   From harmony, from heav'nly harmony
        This universal frame began:
        When Nature underneath a heap
          Of jarring atoms lay,
        And could not heave her head,
      The tuneful voice was heard from high:
        "Arise, ye more than dead."
     Then cold, and hot, and moist, and dry,

In order to their stations leap,
    And Music's pow'r obey.
From harmony, from heav'nly harmony
    This universal frame began:
    From harmony to harmony
Thro' all the compass of the notes it ran,
The diapason closing full in Man.

II   What passion cannot Music raise and quell!
    When Jubal struck the corded shell,
    His list'ning brethren stood around,
    And, wond'ring, on their faces fell
    To worship that celestial sound.
Less than a god they thought there could not dwell
    Within the hollow of that shell
    That spoke so sweetly and so well.
What passion cannot Music raise and quell!

III   The Trumpet's loud clangour
    Excites us to arms,
    With shrill notes of anger,
    And mortal alarms.
    The double double double beat
    Of the thund'ring Drum
Cries: "Hark! the foes come;
Charge, charge, 't is too late to retreat."

IV   The soft complaining Flute
    In dying notes discovers
    The woes of hopeless lovers,
Whose dirge is whisper'd by the warbling Lute.

V   Sharp Violins proclaim
Their jealous pangs, and desperation,
Fury, frantic indignation,
Depth of pains, and height of passion,
    For the fair, disdainful dame.

VI   But O! what art can teach,
          What human voice can reach,
     The sacred Organ's praise?
       Notes inspiring holy love,
     Notes that wing their heav'nly ways
       To mend the choirs above.

VII Orpheus could lead the savage race;
     And trees unrooted left their place,
       Sequacious of the lyre;
     But bright Cecilia rais'd the wonder high'r:
     When to her Organ vocal breath was giv'n,
     An angel heard, and straight appear'd,
       Mistaking earth for heav'n.

Grand Chorus

     As from the pow'r of sacred lays
       The spheres began to move,
     And sung the great Creator's praise
       To all the blest above;
     So, when the last and dreadful hour
     This crumbling pageant shall devour,
     The Trumpet shall be heard on high,
     The dead shall live, the living die,
     And Music shall untune the sky.

PROLOGUE *to* THE MISTAKES OR, THE FALSE REPORT

Enter MR. WILLIAMS

  Save ye, sirs, save ye! I am in a hopeful way,
I should speak something, in rhyme, now, for the play:
But the deuce take me, if I know what to say.
I'll stick to my friend the author, that I can tell ye,
To the last drop of claret in my belly.
So far I'm sure 't is rhyme—that needs no granting:
And, if my verses' feet stumble—you see my own are want-
     ing.
Our young poet has brought a piece of work,
In which, tho' much of art there does not lurk,

It may hold out three days—and that's as long as Cork.
But, for this play—(which till I have done, we show not)
What may be its fortune—by the Lord—I know not.
This I dare swear, no malice here is writ:
'T is innocent of all things; ev'n of wit.
He 's no high-flyer; he makes no sky-rockets,
His squibs are only level'd at your pockets.
And if his crackers light among your pelf,
You are blown up; if not, then he 's blown up himself.
By this time, I 'm something recover'd of my fluster'd
   madness:
And now a word or two in sober sadness.
Ours is a common play; and you pay down
A common harlot's price—just half a crown.
You 'll say, I play the pimp on my friend's score;
But since 't is for a friend, your gibes give o'er:
For many a mother has done that before.
How's this, you cry? an actor write?—we know it;
But Shakespeare was an actor and a poet.
Has not great Jonson's learning often fail'd?
But Shakespeare's greater genius still prevail'd.
Have not some writing actors, in this age,
Deserv'd and found success upon the stage?
To tell the truth, when our old wits are tir'd,
Not one of us but means to be inspir'd.
Let your kind presence grace our homely cheer;
"Peace and the butt" is all our bus'ness here:
So much for that—and the Devil take small beer.

EPILOGUE *to* KING ARTHUR
Spoken by Mrs. Bracegirdle

 I've had to-day a dozen *billets-doux*
From fops, and wits, and cits, and Bow Street *beaux;*
Some from Whitehall, but from the Temple more:
A Covent Garden porter brought me four.
I have not yet read all; but, without feigning,
We maids can make shrewd guesses at your meaning.

What if, to shew your styles, I read 'em here?
Methinks I hear one cry: "O Lord, forbear!
No, madam, no; by Heav'n, that's too severe."
Well then, be safe—
But swear henceforwards to renounce all writing,
And take this solemn oath of my inditing,
As you love ease, and hate campaigns and fighting.
Yet, faith, 't is just to make some few examples:
What if I shew'd you one or two for samples?

[*Pulls one out.*

Here 's one desires my ladyship to meet
At the kind couch above in Bridges Street.
O sharping knave! that would have you know what,
For a poor sneaking treat of chocolate.

[*Pulls out another.*

Now, in the name of luck, I'll break this open,
Because I dreamt last night I had a token:
The superscription is exceeding pretty:
To the desire of all the town and city.
Now, gallants, you must know, this precious fop
Is foreman of a haberdasher's shop:
One who devoutly cheats, demure in carriage,
And courts me to the holy bands of marriage;
But with a civil innuendo too,
My overplus of love shall be for you.

[*Reads.*

"Madam, I swear your looks are so divine,
When I set up, your face shall be my sign:
Tho' times are hard, to shew how I adore you,
Here 's my whole heart, and half a guinea for you.
But have a care of *beaux;* they 're false, my honey;
And, which is worse, have not one rag of money."
    See how maliciously the rogue would wrong ye!
But I know better things of some among ye.
My wisest way will be to keep the stage,
And trust to the good nature of the age;
And he that likes the music and the play
Shall be my favourite gallant to-day.

I. O PASS NOT ON BUT STAY

1 Syren.

O pass not on, but stay,
And waste the joyous day
With us in gentle play:
Unbend to love, unbend thee:
O lay thy sword aside,
And other arms provide;
For other wars attend thee,
And sweeter to be try'd.

Chorus.

For other wars, &c.

Both sing.

Two daughters of this aged stream are we;
And both our sea-green locks have comb'd for thee;
Come bathe with us an hour or two,
Come naked in, for we are so;
What danger from a naked foe?
Come bathe with us, come bathe, and share,
What pleasures in the floods appear;
We'll beat the waters till they bound,
And circle round, around, around,
And circle round, around.

II. HARVEST SONG

Comus.

Your hay it is mow'd, and your corn is reap'd;
Your barns will be full, and your hovels heap'd:
Come, my boys, come;
Come, my boys, come;
And merrily roar out harvest-home;
Harvest-home,
Harvest-home;
And merrily roar out harvest-home.

Chorus.

Come, my boys, come, &c.

First Man.

    We ha' cheated the parson, we 'll cheat him again,
    For why should a blockhead ha' one in ten?
          One in ten,
          One in ten;
    For why should a blockhead ha' one in ten?

Chorus.

          One in ten,
          One in ten;
    For why should a blockhead ha' one in ten?

Second Man.

    For prating so long like a book-learn'd sot,
    Till pudding and dumplin burn to pot;
          Burn to pot,
          Burn to pot;
    Till pudding and dumplin burn to pot.

Chorus.

          Burn to pot, &c.

Third Man.

    We 'll toss off our ale till we canno' stand,
    And hoigh for the honour of old England;
          Old England,
          Old England;
    And hoigh for the honour of old England.

Chorus.

          Old England, &c.

III. SONG SUNG BY VENUS IN HONOUR OF BRITANNIA

    I   Fairest isle, all isles excelling,
          Seat of pleasures and of loves;
      Venus here will choose her dwelling,
          And forsake her Cyprian groves.

    II   Cupid from his fav'rite nation
          Care and envy will remove;
      Jealousy, that poisons passion,
          And despair, that dies for love.

III   Gentle murmurs, sweet complaining,
        Sighs that blow the fire of love;
    Soft repulses, kind disdaining,
        Shall be all the pains you prove.

IV   Every swain shall pay his duty,
        Grateful every nymph shall prove;
    And as these excel in beauty,
        Those shall be renown'd for love.

PROLOGUE: *Gallants, a bashful poet bids me say*

Gallants, a bashful poet bids me say
He 's come to lose his maidenhead to-day.
Be not too fierce, for he 's but green of age,
And ne'er, till now, debauch'd upon the stage.
He wants the suff'ring part of resolution,
And comes with blushes to his execution.
E'er you deflow'r his Muse, he hopes the pit
Will make some settlement upon his wit.
Promise him well, before the play begin,
For he would fain be cozen'd into sin.
'T is not but that he knows you mean to fail;
But, if you leave him after being frail,
He 'll have, at least, a fair pretense to rail;
To call you base, and swear you us'd him ill,
And put you in the new Deserters' Bill.
Lord, what a troop of perjur'd men we see,
Enow to fill another *Mercury*!
But this the ladies may with patience brook:
Theirs are not the first colours you forsook!
He would be loth the beauties to offend;
But, if he should, he 's not too old to mend.
He 's a young plant, in his first year of bearing;
But his friend swears he will be worth the rearing.
His gloss is still upon him; tho' 't is true
He 's yet unripe, yet take him for the blue.
You think an apricot half green is best:
There 's sweet and sour, and one side good at least.

Mangoes and limes, whose nourishment is little,
Tho' not for food, are yet preserv'd for pickle.
So this green writer may pretend, at least,
To whet your stomachs for a better feast.
He makes this difference in the sexes too:
He sells to men, he gives himself to you.
To both he would contribute some delight,
A mere poetical hermaphrodite.
Thus he 's equipp'd, both to be woo'd and woo,
With arms offensive and defensive too:
'T is hard, he thinks, if neither part will do.

VENI CREATOR SPIRITUS
Translated in paraphrase

Creator Spirit, by whose aid
The world's foundations first were laid,
Come visit ev'ry pious mind;
Come pour thy joys on humankind;
From sin and sorrow set us free,
And make thy temples worthy thee.
  O source of uncreated light,
The Father's promis'd Paraclite!
Thrice holy fount, thrice holy fire,
Our hearts with heav'nly love inspire;
Come, and thy sacred unction bring
To sanctify us, while we sing!
  Plenteous of grace, descend from high,
Rich in thy sev'nfold energy,
Thou strength of his almighty hand,
Whose pow'r does heav'n and earth command!
Proceeding Spirit, our defense,
Who dost the gift of tongues dispense,
And crown'st thy gift with eloquence!
  Refine and purge our earthy parts;
But, O, inflame and fire our hearts!
Our frailties help, our vice control,
Submit the senses to the soul;

And when rebellious they are grown,
Then lay thy hand, and hold 'em down.

Chase from our minds th' infernal foe,
And peace, the fruit of love, bestow;
And lest our feet should step astray,
Protect and guide us in the way.

Make us eternal truths receive,
And practice all that we believe:
Give us thyself, that we may see
The Father and the Son, by thee.

Immortal honour, endless fame,
Attend th' Almighty Father's name:
The Savior Son be glorified,
Who for lost man's redemption died;
And equal adoration be,
Eternal Paraclete, to thee.

RONDELAY: *Chloe found Amyntas lying*

    I   Chloe found Amyntas lying,
        All in tears, upon the plain;
    Sighing to himself, and crying:
        "Wretched I, to love in vain!
    Kiss me, dear, before my dying;
        Kiss me once, and ease my pain!"

    II   Sighing to himself, and crying:
        "Wretched I, to love in vain!
    Ever scorning, and denying
        To reward your faithful swain;
    Kiss me, dear, before my dying;
        Kiss me once, and ease my pain.

    III "Ever scorning, and denying
        To reward your faithful swain."—
    Chloe, laughing at his crying,
        Told him that he lov'd in vain.—
    "Kiss me, dear, before my dying;
        Kiss me once, and ease my pain."

IV Chloe, laughing at his crying,
    Told him that he lov'd in vain;
But repenting, and complying,
    When he kiss'd, she kiss'd again:
Kiss'd him up before his dying;
    Kiss'd him up, and eas'd his pain.

TO MY DEAR FRIEND MR. CONGREVE, ON HIS COMEDY CALL'D
THE DOUBLE-DEALER

Well then, the promis'd hour is come at last;
The present age of wit obscures the past:
Strong were our sires, and as they fought they writ,
Conqu'ring with force of arms, and dint of wit;
Theirs was the giant race, before the flood;
And thus, when Charles return'd, our empire stood.
Like Janus he the stubborn soil manur'd,
With rules of husbandry the rankness cur'd;
Tam'd us to manners, when the stage was rude;
And boist'rous English wit with art indued.
Our age was cultivated thus at length,
But what we gain'd in skill we lost in strength.
Our builders were with want of genius curst;
The second temple was not like the first:
Till you, the best Vitruvius, come at length;
Our beauties equal, but excel our strength.
Firm Doric pillars found your solid base;
The fair Corinthian crowns the higher space:
Thus all below is strength, and all above is grace.
In easy dialogue is Fletcher's praise;
He mov'd the mind, but had not power to raise.
Great Jonson did by strength of judgment please;
Yet, doubling Fletcher's force, he wants his ease.
In differing talents both adorn'd their age;
One for the study, t'other for the stage:
But both to Congreve justly shall submit,
One match'd in judgment, both o'ermatch'd in wit.

In him all beauties of this age we see,
Etherege, his courtship, Southerne's purity,
The satire, wit, and strength of Manly Wycherley.
All this in blooming youth you have achiev'd,
Nor are your foil'd contemporaries griev'd.
So much the sweetness of your manners move,
We cannot envy you, because we love.
Fabius might joy in Scipio, when he saw
A beardless consul made against the law;
And join his suffrage to the votes of Rome,
Tho' he with Hannibal was overcome.
Thus old Romano bow'd to Raphael's fame,
And scholar to the youth he taught became.
   O that your brows my laurel had sustain'd;
Well had I been depos'd, if you had reign'd!
The father had descended for the son;
For only you are lineal to the throne.
Thus, when the state one Edward did depose,
A greater Edward in his room arose.
But now, not I, but poetry is curst;
For Tom the Second reigns like Tom the First.
But let 'em not mistake my patron's part,
Nor call his charity their own desert.
Yet this I prophesy: thou shalt be seen
(Tho' with some short parenthesis between)
High on the throne of wit; and, seated there,
Not mine—that 's little—but thy laurel wear.
Thy first attempt an early promise made;
That early promise this has more than paid.
So bold, yet so judiciously you dare,
That your least praise is to be regular.
Time, place, and action, may with pains be wrought;
But genius must be born, and never can be taught.
This is your portion; this your native store;
Heav'n, that but once was prodigal before,
To Shakespeare gave as much; she could not give him more.
   Maintain your post: that's all the fame you need;
For 't is impossible you should proceed.
Already I am worn with cares and age,

And just abandoning th' ungrateful stage;
Unprofitably kept at Heav'n's expense,
I live a rent-charge on his providence;
But you, whom ev'ry Muse and Grace adorn,
Whom I foresee to better fortune born,
Be kind to my remains; and O defend,
Against your judgment, your departed friend!
Let not the insulting foe my fame pursue,
But shade those laurels which descend to you;
And take for tribute what these lines express:
You merit more; nor could my love do less.

PROLOGUE *and* EPILOGUE *from* LOVE TRIUMPHANT
OR, NATURE WILL PREVAIL

PROLOGUE
Spoken by Mr. Betterton

As when some treasurer lays down the stick,
Warrants are sign'd for ready money thick,
And many desperate debentures paid,
Which never had been, had his lordship stay'd;
So now, this poet, who forsakes the stage,
Intends to gratify the present age.
One warrant shall be sign'd for every man;
All shall be wits that will, and beaux that can:
Provided still, this warrant be not shown,
And you be wits but to yourselves alone;
Provided, too, you rail at one another,
For there 's no one wit will allow a brother;
Provided, also, that you spare this story,
Damn all the plays that e'er shall come before ye.
If one by chance prove good in half a score,
Let that one pay for all, and damn it more.
For if a good one scape among the crew,
And you continue judging as you do,
Every bad play will hope for damning too.

You might damn this, if it were worth your pains;
Here 's nothing you will like; no fustian scenes,
And nothing, too, of—you know what he means.
No *double-entendres*, which you sparks allow,
To make the ladies look they know not how;
Simply as 't were, and knowing both together,
Seeming to fan their faces in cold weather.
But here 's a story, which no books relate,
Coin'd from our own old poet's addle-pate.
The fable has a moral, too, if sought;
But let that go; for, upon second thought,
He fears but few come hither to be taught.
Yet if you will be profited, you may;
And he would bribe you too, to like his play.
He dies, at least to us, and to the stage,
And what he has he leaves this noble age.
He leaves you, first, all plays of his inditing,
The whole estate which he has got by writing.
The beaux may think this nothing but vain praise;
They'll find it something, the testator says;
For half their love is made from scraps of plays.
To his worst foes he leaves his honesty,
That they may thrive upon 't as much as he.
He leaves his manners to the roaring boys,
Who come in drunk, and fill the house with noise.
He leaves to the dire critics of his wit,
His silence and contempt of all they writ.
To Shakespeare's critic, he bequeaths the curse,
To find his faults, and yet himself make worse;
A precious reader in poetic schools,
Who by his own examples damns his rules.
Last, for the fair, he wishes you may be,
From your dull critics, the lampooners, free.
Tho' he pretends no legacy to leave you,
An old man may at least good wishes give you.
Your beauty names the play; and may it prove,
To each, an omen of Triumphant Love!

Now, in good manners, nothing should be said
Against this play, because the poet 's dead.
The prologue told us of a moral here:
Would I could find it! but the Devil knows where.
If in my part it lies, I fear he means
To warn us of the sparks behind our scenes.
For, if you 'll take it on Dalinda's word,
'T is a hard chapter to refuse a lord.
The poet might pretend this moral too,
That, when a wit and fool together woo,
The damsel (not to break an ancient rule)
Should leave the wit, and take the wealthy fool.
This he might mean: but there 's a truth behind,
And, since it touches none of all our kind
But masks and misses, faith, I 'll speak my mind.
What if he taught our sex more cautious carriage,
And not to be too coming before marriage;
For fear of my misfortune in the play,
A kid brought home upon the wedding day?
I fear there are few Sanchos in the pit,
So good as to forgive, and to forget;
That will, like him, restore us into favour,
And take us after on our good behaviour.
Few, when they find the money-bag is rent,
Will take it for good payment on content.
But in the telling, there the difference is,
Sometimes they find it more than they could wish.
Therefore be warn'd, you misses and you masks,
Look to your hits, nor give the first that asks.
Tears, sighs, and oaths, no truth of passion prove;
True settlement, alone, declares true love.
For him that weds a puss, who kept her first,
I say but little, but I doubt the worst.
The wife that was a cat may mind her house,
And prove an honest, and a careful spouse;
But, faith, I would not trust her with a mouse.

Once I beheld the fairest of her kind:
(And still the sweet idea charms my mind:)
True, she was dumb; for Nature gaz'd so long,
Pleas'd with her work, that she forgot her tongue,
But, smiling, said: "She still shall gain the prize;
I only have transferr'd it to her eyes."
Such are thy pictures, Kneller: such thy skill,
That Nature seems obedient to thy will;
Comes out, and meets thy pencil in the draught;
Lives there, and wants but words to speak her thought.
At least thy pictures look a voice; and we
Imagine sounds, deceiv'd to that degree,
We think 't is somewhat more than just to see.

    Shadows are but privations of the light;
Yet, when we walk, they shoot before the sight;
With us approach, retire, arise, and fall;
Nothing themselves, and yet expressing all.
Such are thy pieces, imitating life
So near, they almost conquer'd in the strife;
And from their animated canvas came,
Demanding souls, and loosen'd from the frame.

    Prometheus, were he here, would cast away
His Adam, and refuse a soul to clay;
And either would thy noble work inspire,
Or think it warm enough without his fire.

    But vulgar hands may vulgar likeness raise;
This is the least attendant on thy praise:
From hence the rudiments of art began;
A coal, or chalk, first imitated man:
Perhaps the shadow, taken on a wall,
Gave outlines to the rude original;
Ere canvas yet was strain'd, before the grace
Of blended colours found their use and place,
Or cypress tablets first receiv'd a face.

    By slow degrees, the godlike art advanc'd;
As man grew polish'd, picture was inhanc'd:
Greece added posture, shade, and perspective;

And then the mimic piece began to live.
Yet perspective was lame, no distance true,
But all came forward in one common view:
No point of light was known, no bounds of art;
When light was there, it knew not to depart,
But glaring on remoter objects play'd;
Not languish'd and insensibly decay'd.

Rome rais'd not art, but barely kept alive,
And with old Greece unequally did strive;
Till Goths and Vandals, a rude northern race,
Did all the matchless monuments deface.
Then all the Muses in one ruin lie,
And rhyme began t' enervate poetry.
Thus, in a stupid military state,
The pen and pencil find an equal fate.
Flat faces, such as would disgrace a screen,
Such as in Bantam's embassy were seen,
Unrais'd, unrounded, were the rude delight
Of brutal nations, only born to fight.

Long time the sister arts, in iron sleep,
A heavy sabbath did supinely keep:
At length, in Raphael's age, at once they rise,
Stretch all their limbs, and open all their eyes.

Thence rose the Roman and the Lombard line;
One colour'd best, and one did best design.
Raphael's, like Homer's, was the nobler part,
But Titian's painting look'd like Virgil's art.

Thy genius gives thee both; where true design,
Postures unforc'd, and lively colours join.
Likeness is ever there; but still the best,
Like proper thoughts in lofty language dress'd:
Where light, to shades descending, plays, not strives,
Dies by degrees, and by degrees revives.
Of various parts a perfect whole is wrought:
Thy pictures think, and we divine their thought.

Shakespeare,* thy gift, I place before my sight;
With awe, I ask his blessing ere I write;

*Shakespeare's picture, drawn by Sir Godfrey Kneller and given to the author.

With reverence look on his majestic face;
Proud to be less, but of his godlike race.
His soul inspires me, while thy praise I write,
And I, like Teucer, under Ajax fight:
Bids thee, thro' me, be bold; with dauntless breast
Contemn the bad, and emulate the best.
Like his, thy critics in th' attempt are lost:
When most they rail, know then, they envy most.
In vain they snarl aloof; a noisy crowd,
Like women's anger, impotent and loud.
While they their barren industry deplore,
Pass on secure, and mind the goal before.
Old as she is, my Muse shall march behind,
Bear off the blast, and intercept the wind.
Our arts are sisters, tho' not twins in birth;
For hymns were sung in Eden's happy earth
By the first pair, while Eve was yet a saint,
Before she fell with pride, and learn'd to paint.
Forgive th' allusion; 't was not meant to bite,
But satire will have room, where'er I write.
For O the painter Muse, tho' last in place,
Has seiz'd the blessing first, like Jacob's race.
Apelles' art an Alexander found,
And Raphael did with Leo's gold abound;
But Homer was with barren laurel crown'd.
Thou hadst thy Charles a while, and so had I;
But pass we that unpleasing image by.
Rich in thyself, and of thyself divine,
All pilgrims come and offer at thy shrine.
A graceful truth thy pencil can command:
The fair themselves go mended from thy hand.
Likeness appears in every lineament;
But likeness in thy work is eloquent.
Tho' Nature there her true resemblance bears,
A nobler beauty in thy piece appears.
So warm thy work, so glows the gen'rous frame,
Flesh looks less living in the lovely dame.
Thou paint'st as we describe, improving still,
When on wild nature we ingraft our skill;

But not creating beauties at our will.

Some other hand perhaps may reach a face,
But none like thee a finish'd figure place:
None of this age; for that 's enough for thee,
The first of these inferior times to be,
Not to contend with heroes' memory.
Due honours to those mighty names we grant,
But shrubs may live beneath the lofty plant;
Sons may succeed their greater parents gone:
Such is thy lot, and such I wish my own.

But poets are confin'd in narr'wer space,
To speak the language of their native place:
The painter widely stretches his command;
Thy pencil speaks the tongue of ev'ry land.
From hence, my friend, all climates are your own,
Nor can you forfeit, for you hold of none.
All nations all immunities will give
To make you theirs, where'er you please to live;
And not seven cities, but the world would strive.

Sure some propitious planet then did smile,
When first you were conducted to this isle:
Our genius brought you here, t' inlarge our fame,
For your good stars are ev'rywhere the same.
Thy matchless hand, of ev'ry region free,
Adopts our climate, not our climate thee.

Great Rome and Venice** early did impart
To thee th' examples of their wondrous art.
Those masters then, but seen, not understood,
With generous emulation fir'd thy blood;
For what in nature's dawn the child admir'd,
The youth endeavour'd, and the man acquir'd.

That yet thou hast not reach'd their high degree,
Seems only wanting to this age, not thee.
Thy genius, bounded by the times, like mine,
Drudges on petty draughts, nor dare design
A more exalted work, and more divine.
For what a song, or senseless opera
Is to the living labour of a play;

**He travel'd very young into Italy.

‡77‡

Or what a play to Virgil's work would be,
Such is a single piece to history.

But we, who life bestow, ourselves must live;
Kings cannot reign unless their subjects give;
And they who pay the taxes bear the rule:
Thus thou, sometimes, art forc'd to draw a fool;
But so his follies in thy posture sink,
The senseless idiot seems at least to think.

Good Heav'n! that sots and knaves should be so vain,
To wish their vile resemblance may remain!
And stand recorded, at their own request,
To future days, a libel or a jest!
Meantime, while just incouragement you want,
You only paint to live, not live to paint.

Else should we see your noble pencil trace
Our unities of action, time, and place;
A whole compos'd of parts, and those the best,
With ev'ry various character express'd;
Heroes at large, and at a nearer view;
Less, and at distance, an ignobler crew;
While all the figures in one action join,
As tending to complete the main design.

More cannot be by mortal art express'd,
But venerable age shall add the rest:
For Time shall with his ready pencil stand;
Retouch your figures with his ripening hand;
Mellow your colours, and imbrown the teint;
Add every grace, which Time alone can grant;
To future ages shall your fame convey,
And give more beauties than he takes away.

ALEXANDER'S FEAST OR, THE POWER OF MUSIC;
AN ODE IN HONOUR OF ST. CECILIA'S DAY

1   'T was at the royal feast, for Persia won
              By Philip's warlike son:
          Aloft in awful state
          The godlike hero sate
              On his imperial throne:

His valiant peers were plac'd around;
Their brows with roses and with myrtles bound:
 (So should desert in arms be crown'd.)
The lovely Thais, by his side,
Sate like a blooming Eastern bride
In flow'r of youth and beauty's pride.
 Happy, happy, happy pair!
 None but the brave,
 None but the brave,
 None but the brave deserves the fair.

Chorus

> *Happy, happy, happy pair!*
> *None but the brave,*
> *None but the brave,*
> *None but the brave deserves the fair.*

II Timotheus, plac'd on high
 Amid the tuneful choir,
 With flying fingers touch'd the lyre:
The trembling notes ascend the sky,
   And heav'nly joys inspire.
The song began from Jove,
Who left his blissful seats above,
(Such is the pow'r of mighty love.)
A dragon's fiery form belied the god:
Sublime on radiant spires he rode,
 When he to fair Olympia press'd;
 And while he sought her snowy breast:
Then, round her slender waist he curl'd,
And stamp'd an image of himself, a sov'reign
  of the world.
The list'ning crowd admire the lofty sound;
"A present deity," they shout around;
"A present deity," the vaulted roofs rebound:
  With ravish'd ears
  The monarch hears,
  Assumes the god,
  Affects to nod,
 And seems to shake the spheres.

> *With ravish'd ears*
> *The monarch hears,*
> *Assumes the god,*
> *Affects to nod,*
> *And seems to shake the spheres.*

III   The praise of Bacchus then the sweet musician sung,
     Of Bacchus ever fair and ever young:
       The jolly god in triumph comes;
       Sound the trumpets; beat the drums;
         Flush'd with a purple grace
         He shews his honest face:
Now give the hautboys breath; he comes, he comes.
       Bacchus, ever fair and young,
         Drinking joys did first ordain;
       Bacchus' blessings are a treasure,
       Drinking is the soldier's pleasure:
         Rich the treasure,
         Sweet the pleasure,
       Sweet is pleasure after pain.

Chorus

> *Bacchus' blessings are a treasure,*
> *Drinking is the soldier's pleasure:*
>   *Rich the treasure,*
>   *Sweet the pleasure,*
> *Sweet is pleasure after pain.*

IV   Sooth'd with the sound, the king grew vain;
     Fought all his battles o'er again;
And thrice he routed all his foes; and thrice he slew
     the slain.
The master saw the madness rise;
His glowing cheeks, his ardent eyes;
And, while he heav'n and earth defied,
Chang'd his hand, and check'd his pride.
     He chose a mournful Muse,
        Soft pity to infuse:

He sung Darius great and good,
  By too severe a fate,
Fallen, fallen, fallen, fallen,
    Fallen from his high estate,
      And welt'ring in his blood;
Deserted, at his utmost need,
By those his former bounty fed;
On the bare earth expos'd he lies,
With not a friend to close his eyes.

With downcast looks the joyless victor sate,
  Revolving in his alter'd soul
    The various turns of chance below;
  And, now and then, a sigh he stole;
    And tears began to flow.

Chorus

  Revolving in his alter'd soul
    The various turns of chance below;
  And, now and then, a sigh he stole;
    And tears began to flow.

v The mighty master smil'd, to see
   That love was in the next degree:
   'T was but a kindred sound to move,
   For pity melts the mind to love.
     Softly sweet, in Lydian measures,
     Soon he sooth'd his soul to pleasures.
     "War," he sung, "is toil and trouble;
     Honour, but an empty bubble;
       Never ending, still beginning,
     Fighting still, and still destroying:
       If the world be worth thy winning,
     Think, O think it worth enjoying;
       Lovely Thais sits beside thee,
       Take the good the gods provide thee."

The many rend the skies with loud applause:
So Love was crown'd, but Music won the cause.

The prince, unable to conceal his pain,
    Gaz'd on the fair
    Who caus'd his care,
  And sigh'd and look'd, sigh'd and look'd,
Sigh'd and look'd, and sigh'd again:
At length, with love and wine at once oppress'd,
The vanquish'd victor sunk upon her breast.

Chorus

> *The prince, unable to conceal his pain,*
>   *Gaz'd on the fair*
>   *Who caus'd his care,*
>   *And sigh'd and look'd, sigh'd and look'd,*
> *Sigh'd and look'd, and sigh'd again:*
> *At length, with love and wine at once oppress'd,*
> *The vanquish'd victor sunk upon her breast.*

VI Now strike the golden lyre again:
A louder yet, and yet a louder strain.
Break his bands of sleep asunder,
And rouse him, like a rattling peal of thunder.
    Hark, hark, the horrid sound
      Has rais'd up his head:
      As awak'd from the dead,
    And amaz'd, he stares around.
"Revenge, revenge!" Timotheus cries,
    "See the Furies arise!
  See the snakes that they rear,
  How they hiss in their hair,
And the sparkles that flash from their eyes!
  Behold a ghastly band,
  Each a torch in his hand!
Those are Grecian ghosts, that in battle were slain,
    And unburied remain
    Inglorious on the plain:
    Give the vengeance due
    To the valiant crew.
Behold how they toss their torches on high,
  How they point to the Persian abodes,
And glitt'ring temples of their hostile gods!"

The princes applaud, with a furious joy;
And the king seiz'd a flambeau with zeal to destroy;
    Thais led the way,
    To light him to his prey,
And, like another Helen, fir'd another Troy.

Chorus

> *And the king seiz'd a flambeau with zeal to destroy;*
>   *Thais led the way,*
>   *To light him to his prey,*
> *And, like another Helen, fir'd another Troy.*

VII   Thus, long ago,
    Ere heaving bellows learn'd to blow,
      White organs yet were mute;
    Timotheus, to his breathing flute,
      And sounding lyre,
Could swell the soul to rage, or kindle soft desire.
    At last, divine Cecilia came,
    Inventress of the vocal frame;
The sweet enthusiast, from her sacred store,
    Enlarg'd the former narrow bounds,
    And added length to solemn sounds,
With nature's mother wit, and arts unknown before.
    Let old Timotheus yield the prize,
    Or both divide the crown;
    He rais'd a mortal to the skies;
    She drew an angel down.

Grand Chorus

> *At last, divine Cecilia came,*
> *Inventress of the vocal frame;*
> *The sweet enthusiast, from her sacred store,*
>   *Enlarg'd the former narrow bounds,*
>   *And added length to solemn sounds,*
> *With nature's mother wit, and arts unknown before.*
>   *Let old Timotheus yield the prize,*
>   *Or both divide the crown;*
>   *He rais'd a mortal to the skies;*
>   *She drew an angel down.*

'T is hard, my friend, to write in such an age,
As damns not only poets, but the stage.
That sacred art, by heav'n itself infus'd,
Which Moses, David, Solomon have us'd,
Is now to be no more: the Muses' foes
Would sink their Maker's praises into prose.
Were they content to prune the lavish vine
Of straggling branches, and improve the wine,
Who but a madman would his faults defend?
All would submit; for all but fools will mend.
But when to common sense they give the lie,
And turn distorted words to blasphemy,
They give the scandal; and the wise discern,
Their glosses teach an age too apt to learn.
What I have loosely or profanely writ,
Let them to fires, (their due desert,) commit;
Nor, when accus'd by me, let *them* complain:
Their faults and not their function I arraign.
Rebellion, worse than witchcraft, they pursued;
The pulpit preach'd the crime, the people rued.
The stage was silenc'd; for the saints would see
In fields perform'd their plotted tragedy.
But let us first reform, and then so live,
That we may teach our teachers to forgive.
Our desk be plac'd below their lofty chairs;
Ours be the practice, as the precept theirs.
The moral part at least we may divide,
Humility reward, and punish pride;
Ambition, int'rest, avarice accuse:
These are the province of the Tragic Muse.
These hast thou chosen; and the public voice
Has equal'd thy performance with thy choice.
Time, action, place, are so preserv'd by thee,
That ev'n Corneille might with envy see
Th' alliance of his tripled unity.
Thy incidents, perhaps, too thick are sown;
But too much plenty is thy fault alone:

At least but two can that good crime commit,
Thou in design, and Wycherley in wit.
Let thy own Gauls condemn thee, if they dare;
Contented to be thinly regular.
Born there, but not for them, our fruitful soil
With more increase rewards thy happy toil.
Their tongue, infeebled, is refin'd so much,
That, like pure gold, it bends at ev'ry touch;
Our sturdy Teuton yet will art obey,
More fit for manly thought, and strengthen'd with allay.
But whence art thou inspir'd, and thou alone,
To flourish in an idiom not thine own?
It moves our wonder, that a foreign guest
Should overmatch the most, and match the best.
In underpraising, thy deserts I wrong;
Here, find the first deficience of our tongue:
Words, once my stock, are wanting, to commend
So great a poet and so good a friend.

TO HER GRACE THE DUCHESS OF ORMOND WITH THE FOLLOWING POEM OF PALAMON AND ARCITE FROM CHAUCER

   Madam,
The bard who first adorn'd our native tongue,
Tun'd to his British lyre this ancient song;
Which Homer might without a blush rehearse,
And leaves a doubtful palm in Virgil's verse:
He match'd their beauties, where they most excel;
Of love sung better, and of arms as well.

   Vouchsafe, illustrious Ormond, to behold
What pow'r the charms of beauty had of old;
Nor wonder if such deeds of arms were done,
Inspir'd by two fair eyes, that sparkled like your own.

   If Chaucer by the best idea wrought,
And poets can divine each other's thought,
The fairest nymph before his eyes he set;
And then the fairest was Plantagenet;
Who three contending princes made her prize,

And rul'd the rival nations with her eyes;
Who left immortal trophies of her fame,
And to the noblest order gave the name.

Like her, of equal kindred to the throne,
You keep her conquests, and extend your own:
As when the stars, in their ethereal race,
At length have roll'd around the liquid space,
At certain periods they resume their place,
From the same point of heav'n their course advance,
And move in measures of their former dance;
Thus, after length of ages, she returns,
Restor'd in you, and the same place adorns;
Or you perform her office in the sphere,
Born of her blood, and make a new Platonic year.

O true Plantagenet, O race divine,
(For beauty still is fatal to the line,)
Had Chaucer liv'd that angel face to view,
Sure he had drawn his Emily from you;
Or had you liv'd to judge the doubtful right,
Your noble Palamon had been the knight;
And conqu'ring Theseus from his side had sent
Your gen'rous lord, to guide the Theban government.

Time shall accomplish that; and I shall see
A Palamon in him, in you an Emily.

Already have the Fates your path prepar'd,
And sure presage your future sway declar'd:
When westward, like the sun, you took your way,
And from benighted Britain bore the day,
Blue Triton gave the signal from the shore,
The ready Nereids heard, and swam before,
To smooth the seas; a soft Etesian gale
But just inspir'd, and gently swell'd the sail;
Portunus took his turn, whose ample hand
Heav'd up the lighten'd keel, and sunk the sand,
And steer'd the sacred vessel safe to land.
The land, if not restrain'd, had met your way,
Projected out a neck, and jutted to the sea.
Hibernia, prostrate at your feet, ador'd,
In you, the pledge of her expected lord,

Due to her isle; a venerable name;
His father and his grandsire known to fame:
Aw'd by that house, accustom'd to command,
The sturdy kerns in due subjection stand,
Nor hear the reins in any foreign hand.

At your approach, they crowded to the port;
And scarcely landed, you create a court:
As Ormond's harbinger, to you they run;
For Venus is the promise of the sun.

The waste of civil wars, their towns destroy'd,
Pales unhonour'd, Ceres unemploy'd,
Were all forgot; and one triumphant day
Wip'd all the tears of three campaigns away.
Blood, rapines, massacres, were cheaply bought,
So mighty recompense your beauty brought.

As when the dove returning bore the mark
Of earth restor'd to the long-lab'ring ark,
The relics of mankind, secure of rest,
Op'd ev'ry window to receive the guest,
And the fair bearer of the message bless'd;
So, when you came, with loud repeated cries,
The nation took an omen from your eyes,
And God advanc'd his rainbow in the skies,
To sign inviolable peace restor'd;
The saints, with solemn shouts, proclaim'd the new
            accord.

When at your second coming you appear,
(For I foretell that millenary year,)
The sharpen'd share shall vex the soil no more,
But earth unbidden shall produce her store;
The land shall laugh, the circling ocean smile,
And Heav'n's indulgence bless the holy isle.

Heav'n from all ages has reserv'd for you
That happy clime which venom never knew:
Or if it had been there, your eyes alone
Have pow'r to chase all poison but their own.

Now in this interval, which fate has cast
Betwixt your future glories and your past,
This pause of pow'r, 't is Ireland's hour to mourn,

While England celebrates your safe return,
By which you seem the seasons to command,
And bring our summers back to their forsaken land.
  The vanquish'd isle our leisure must attend,
Till the fair blessing we vouchsafe to send;
Nor can we spare you long, tho' often we may lend.
The dove was twice employ'd abroad, before
The world was dried and she return'd no more.

  Nor dare we trust so soft a messenger,
New from her sickness, to that northern air;
Rest here a while your lustre to restore,
That they may see you as you shone before,
For yet, th' eclipse not wholly past, you wade
Thro' some remains, and dimness of a shade.

  A subject in his prince may claim a right,
Nor suffer him with strength impair'd to fight;
Till force returns, his ardour we restrain,
And curb his warlike wish to cross the main.

  Now past the danger, let the learn'd begin
Th' enquiry where disease could enter in;
How those malignant atoms forc'd their way,
What in the faultless frame they found to make their
       prey;
Where ev'ry element was weigh'd so well,
That Heav'n alone, who mix'd the mass, could tell
Which of the four ingredients could rebel;
And where, imprison'd in so sweet a cage,
A soul might well be pleas'd to pass an age.

  And yet the fine materials made it weak;
Porcelain, by being pure, is apt to break:
Ev'n to your breast the sickness durst aspire;
And, forc'd from that fair temple to retire,
Profanely set the holy place on fire.
In vain your lord, like young Vespasian, mourn'd,
When the fierce flames the sanctuary burn'd;
And I prepar'd to pay in verses rude
A most detested act of gratitude:
Ev'n this had been your elegy, which now
Is offer'd for your health, the table of my vow.

Your angel sure our Morley's mind inspir'd,
To find the remedy your ill requir'd;
As once the Macedon, by Jove's decree,
Was taught to dream an herb for Ptolomee:
Or Heav'n, which had such over-cost bestow'd,
As scarce it could afford to flesh and blood,
So lik'd the frame, he would not work anew,
To save the charges of another you.
Or by his middle science did he steer,
And saw some great contingent good appear,
Well worth a miracle to keep you here;
And, for that end, preserv'd the precious mould,
Which all the future Ormonds was to hold;
And meditated in his better mind
An heir from you, who may redeem the failing kind.

Blest be the pow'r which has at once restor'd
The hopes of lost succession to your lord;
Joy to the first and last of each degree,
Virtue to courts, and, what I long'd to see,
To you the Graces, and the Muse to me.

O daughter of the rose, whose cheeks unite
The diff'ring titles of the red and white;
Who heav'n's alternate beauty well display,
The blush of morning, and the milky way,
Whose face is paradise, but fenc'd from sin:
For God in either eye has plac'd a cherubin.

All is your lord's alone; ev'n absent, he
Employs the care of chaste Penelope.
For him you waste in tears your widow'd hours,
For him your curious needle paints the flow'rs;
Such works of old imperial dames were taught;
Such, for Ascanius, fair Elisa wrought.

The soft recesses of your hours improve
The three fair pledges of your happy love:
All other parts of pious duty done,
You owe your Ormond nothing but a son;
To fill in future times his father's place,
And wear the garter of his mother's race.

How blest is he, who leads a country life,
Unvex'd with anxious cares, and void of strife!
Who, studying peace and shunning civil rage,
Enjoy'd his youth, and now enjoys his age:
All who deserve his love, he makes his own;
And, to be lov'd himself, needs only to be known.

Just, good, and wise, contending neighbours come,
From your award to wait their final doom;
And, foes before, return in friendship home.
Without their cost, you terminate the cause,
And save th' expense of long litigious laws:
Where suits are travers'd, and so little won,
That he who conquers is but last undone.
Such are not your decrees; but so design'd,
The sanction leaves a lasting peace behind:
Like your own soul, serene; a pattern of your mind.

Promoting concord, and composing strife,
Lord of yourself, uncumber'd with a wife;
Where, for a year, a month, perhaps a night,
Long penitence succeeds a short delight:
Minds are so hardly match'd, that ev'n the first,
Tho' pair'd by Heav'n, in Paradise were curst.
For man and woman, tho' in one they grow,
Yet, first or last, return again to two.
He to God's image, she to his was made;
So, farther from the fount, the stream at random stray'd.

How could he stand, when, put to double pain,
He must a weaker than himself sustain!
Each might have stood perhaps, but each alone;
Two wrestlers help to pull each other down.

Not that my verse would blemish all the fair;
But yet if *some* be bad, 't is wisdom to beware;
And better shun the bait than struggle in the snare.
Thus have you shunn'd, and shun, the married state,
Trusting as little as you can to fate.

No porter guards the passage of your door,

T' admit the wealthy, and exclude the poor;
For God, who gave the riches, gave the heart,
To sanctify the whole, by giving part.
Heav'n, who foresaw the will, the means has wrought,
And to the second son a blessing brought;
The first-begotten had his father's share,
But you, like Jacob, are Rebecca's heir.

So may your stores and fruitful fields increase;
And ever be you blest, who live to bless.
As Ceres sow'd, where'er her chariot flew;
As Heav'n in desarts rain'd the bread of dew;
So free to many, to relations most,
You feed with manna your own Israel host.

With crowds attended of your ancient race,
You seek the champian sports or sylvan chase;
With well-breath'd beagles you surround the wood,
Ev'n then industrious of the common good;
And often have you brought the wily fox
To suffer for the firstlings of the flocks;
Chas'd ev'n amid the folds, and made to bleed,
Like felons, where they did the murd'rous deed.
This fiery game your active youth maintain'd,
Not yet by years extinguish'd, tho' restrain'd:
You season still with sports your serious hours;
For age but tastes of pleasures, youth devours.
The hare in pastures or in plains is found,
Emblem of human life, who runs the round;
And after all his wand'ring ways are done,
His circle fills and ends where he begun,
Just as the setting meets the rising sun.

Thus princes ease their cares; but happier he
Who seeks not pleasure thro' necessity,
Than such as once on slipp'ry thrones were plac'd;
And chasing, sigh to think themselves are chas'd.

So liv'd our sires, ere doctors learn'd to kill,
And multiplied with theirs the weekly bill.
The first physicians by debauch were made;
Excess began, and sloth sustains the trade.
Pity the gen'rous kind their cares bestow

To search forbidden truths; (a sin to know:)
To which if human science could attain,
The doom of death, pronounc'd by God, were vain.
In vain the leech would interpose delay;
Fate fastens first, and vindicates the prey.
What help from art's endeavours can we have?
Gibbons but guesses, nor is sure to save;
But Maurus sweeps whole parishes, and peoples ev'ry
        grave;
And no more mercy to mankind will use,
Than when he robb'd and murder'd Maro's Muse.
Wouldst thou be soon dispatch'd, and perish whole?
Trust Maurus with thy life, and M-lb-rne with thy soul.

  By chase our long-liv'd fathers earn'd their food;
Toil strung the nerves and purified the blood:
But we, their sons, a pamper'd race of men,
Are dwindled down to threescore years and ten.
Better to hunt in fields for health unbought
Than fee the doctor for a nauseous draught.
The wise for cure on exercise depend;
God never made his work for man to mend.

  The tree of knowledge, once in Eden plac'd,
Was easy found, but was forbid the taste:
O had our grandsire walk'd without his wife,
He first had sought the better plant of life!
Now, both are lost; yet, wand'ring in the dark,
Physicians, for the tree, have found the bark.
They, lab'ring for relief of humankind,
With sharpen'd sight some remedies may find;
Th' apothecary train is wholly blind.
From files a random recipe they take,
And many deaths of one prescription make.
Garth, gen'rous as his Muse, prescribes and gives;
The shopman sells, and by destruction lives:
Ungrateful tribe! who, like the viper's brood,
From med'cine issuing, suck their mother's blood!
Let these obey, and let the learn'd prescribe,
That men may die without a double bribe:
Let them but under their superiors kill,

When doctors first have sign'd the bloody bill;
He scapes the best, who, nature to repair,
Draws physic from the fields, in draughts of vital air.

You hoard not health for your own private use,
But on the public spend the rich produce;
When, often urg'd, unwilling to be great,
Your country calls you from your lov'd retreat,
And sends to senates, charg'd with common care,
Which none more shuns, and none can better bear.
Where could they find another form'd so fit,
To poise with solid sense a sprightly wit?
Were these both wanting, (as they both abound,)
Where could so firm integrity be found?

Well-born, and wealthy, wanting no support,
You steer betwixt the country and the court;
Nor gratify whate'er the great desire,
Nor grudging give what public needs require.
Part must be left, a fund when foes invade;
And part employ'd to roll the wat'ry trade:
Ev'n Canaan's happy land, when worn with toil,
Requir'd a sabbath year to mend the meagre soil.

Good senators (and such are you) so give,
That kings may be supplied, the people thrive.
And he, when want requires, is truly wise,
Who slights not foreign aids, nor overbuys,
But on our native strength, in time of need, relies.
Munster was bought, we boast not the success;
Who fights for gain, for greater makes his peace.

Our foes, compell'd by need, have peace embrac'd;
The peace both parties want is like to last:
Which if secure, securely we may trade;
Or, not secure, should never have been made.
Safe in ourselves, while on ourselves we stand,
The sea is ours, and that defends the land.
Be, then, the naval stores the nation's care,
New ships to build, and batter'd to repair.

Observe the war, in ev'ry annual course;
What has been done was done with British force:
Namur subdued is England's palm alone;

The rest besieg'd, but we constrain'd the town:
We saw th' event that follow'd our success;
France, tho' pretending arms, pursued the peace;
Oblig'd, by one sole treaty, to restore
What twenty years of war had won before.
Enough for Europe has our Albion fought:
Let us enjoy the peace our blood has bought.
When once the Persian king was put to flight,
The weary Macedons refus'd to fight,
Themselves their own mortality confess'd,
And left the son of Jove to quarrel for the rest.

Ev'n victors are by victories undone;
Thus Hannibal, with foreign laurels won,
To Carthage was recall'd, too late to keep his own.
While sore of battle, while our wounds are green,
Why should we tempt the doubtful die again?
In wars renew'd, uncertain of success;
Sure of a share, as umpires of the peace.

A patriot both the king and country serves;
Prerogative and privilege preserves:
Of each our laws the certain limit show;
One must not ebb, nor t'other overflow.
Betwixt the prince and parliament we stand;
The barriers of the state on either hand:
May neither overflow, for then they drown the land!
When both are full, they feed our blest abode;
Like those that water'd once the paradise of God.

Some overpoise of sway by turns they share;
In peace the people, and the prince in war:
Consuls of mod'rate pow'r in calms were made;
When the Gauls came, one sole dictator sway'd.

Patriots, in peace, assert the people's right;
With noble stubbornness resisting might:
No lawless mandates from the court receive,
Nor lend by force, but in a body give.
Such was your gen'rous grandsire; free to grant
In parliaments that weigh'd their prince's want:
But so tenacious of the common cause,
As not to lend the king against his laws;

And, in a loathsome dungeon doom'd to lie,
In bonds retain'd his birthright liberty,
And sham'd oppression, till it set him free.
 O true descendant of a patriot line,
Who, while thou shar'st their lustre, lend'st 'em thine,
Vouchsafe this picture of thy soul to see;
'T is so far good, as it resembles thee.
The beauties to th' original I owe;
Which when I miss, my own defects I show:
Nor think the kindred Muses thy disgrace;
A poet is not born in ev'ry race.
Two of a house few ages can afford;
One to perform, another to record.
Praiseworthy actions are by thee embrac'd;
And 't is my praise, to make thy praises last.
For ev'n when death dissolves our human frame,
The soul returns to heav'n, from whence it came;
Earth keeps the body, verse preserves the fame.

BAUCIS AND PHILEMON
OUT OF THE EIGHTH BOOK OF OVID'S METAMORPHOSES

The author, pursuing the deeds of Theseus, relates how he with his friend
Perithous were invited by Acheloüs, the river god, to stay with him till
his waters were abated. Acheloüs entertains them with a relation of his
own love to Perimele, who was chang'd into an island by Neptune at his
request. Perithous, being an atheist, derides the legend, and denies the
power of the gods to work that miracle. Lelex, another companion of
Theseus, to confirm the story of Acheloüs, relates another metamorphosis
of Baucis and Philemon into trees; of which he was partly an eye witness.

Thus Acheloüs ends: his audience hear
With admiration, and, admiring, fear
The pow'rs of heav'n; except Ixion's son,
Who laugh'd at all the gods, believ'd in none.
He shook his impious head, and thus replies:
"These legends are no more than pious lies:
You attribute too much to heavenly sway,
To think they give us forms, and take away."

The rest, of better minds, their sense declar'd
Against this doctrine, and with horror heard.
Then Lelex rose, an old experienc'd man,
And thus with sober gravity began:
"Heav'n's pow'r is infinite; earth, air, and sea,
The manufactur'd mass, the making pow'r obey.
By proof to clear your doubt: in Phrygian ground
Two neighb'ring trees, with walls encompass'd round,
Stand on a mod'rate rise, with wonder shown,
One a hard oak, a softer linden one:
I saw the place and them, by Pittheus sent
To Phrygian realms, my grandsire's government.
Not far from thence is seen a lake, the haunt
Of coots, and of the fishing cormorant:
Here Jove with Hermes came; but in disguise
Of mortal men conceal'd their deities:
One laid aside his thunder, one his rod;
And many toilsome steps together trod;
For harbour at a thousand doors they knock'd—
Not one of all the thousand but was lock'd.
At last an hopitable house they found,
A homely shed; the roof, not far from ground,
Was thatch'd with reeds and straw together bound.
There Baucis and Philemon liv'd, and there
Had liv'd long married and a happy pair:
Now old in love; tho' little was their store,
Inur'd to want, their poverty they bore,
Nor aim'd at wealth, professing to be poor.
For master or for servant here to call,
Was all alike, where only two were all.
Command was none, where equal love was paid,
Or rather both commanded, both obey'd.
    "From lofty roofs the gods repuls'd before,
Now, stooping, enter'd thro' the little door;
The man (their hearty welcome first express'd)
A common settle drew for either guest,
Inviting each his weary limbs to rest.
But ere they sat, officious Baucis lays
Two cushions stuff'd with straw, the seat to raise;

Coarse, but the best she had; then rakes the load
Of ashes from the hearth, and spreads abroad
The living coals, and, lest they should expire,
With leaves and barks she feeds her infant fire:
It smokes, and then with trembling breath she blows,
Till in a cheerful blaze the flames arose.
With brushwood and with chips she strengthens these,
And adds at last the boughs of rotten trees.
The fire thus form'd, she sets the kettle on—
Like burnish'd gold the little seether shone—
Next took the coleworts which her husband got
From his own ground (a small well-water'd spot);
She stripp'd the stalks of all their leaves; the best
She cull'd, and then with handy care she dress'd.
High o'er the hearth a chine of bacon hung:
Good old Philemon seiz'd it with a prong,
And from the sooty rafter drew it down;
Then cut a slice, but scarce enough for one;
Yet a large portion of a little store,
Which for their sakes alone he wish'd were more.
This in the pot he plung'd without delay,
To tame the flesh and drain the salt away.
The time between, before the fire they sat,
And shorten'd the delay by pleasing chat.
    "A beam there was, on which a beechen pail
Hung by the handle, on a driven nail:
This fill'd with water, gently warm'd, they set
Before their guests; in this they bath'd their feet,
And after with clean towels dried their sweat.
This done, the host produc'd the genial bed,
Sallow the feet, the borders, and the stead,
Which with no costly coverlet they spread,
But coarse old garments; yet such robes as these
They laid alone, at feasts, on holidays.
The good old housewife, tucking up her gown,
The table sets; th' invited gods lie down.
The trivet table of a foot was lame —
A blot which prudent Baucis overcame,
Who thrusts beneath the limping leg a sherd;

So was the mended board exactly rear'd:
Then rubb'd it o'er with newly gather'd mint,
A wholesome herb, that breath'd a grateful scent.
Pallas began the feast, where first was seen
The party-colour'd olive, black and green;
Autumnal cornels next in order serv'd,
In lees of wine well pickled and preserv'd;
A garden salad was the third supply,
Of endive, radishes, and succory;
Then curds and cream, the flow'r of country fare,
And new-laid eggs, which Baucis' busy care
Turn'd by a gentle fire, and roasted rear.
All these in earthenware were serv'd to board;
And, next in place, an earthen pitcher, stor'd
With liquor of the best the cottage could afford.
This was the table's ornament and pride,
With figures wrought: like pages at his side
Stood beechen bowls; and these were shining clean,
Vernish'd with wax without, and lin'd within.
By this the boiling kettle had prepar'd
And to the table sent the smoking lard,
On which with eager appetite they dine,
A savr'y bit, that serv'd to relish wine;
The wine itself was suiting to the rest,
Still working in the must, and lately press'd.
The second course succeeds like that before;
Plums, apples, nuts, and, of their wintry store,
Dry figs and grapes, and wrinkled dates were set
In canisters, t' enlarge the little treat.
All these a milk-white honeycomb surround,
Which in the midst the country banquet crown'd.
But the kind hosts their entertainment grace
With hearty welcome, and an open face:
In all they did you might discern with ease
A willing mind, and a desire to please.
    "Meantime the beechen bowls went round, and still,
Tho' often emptied, were observ'd to fill;
Fill'd without hands, and of their own accord
Ran without feet, and danc'd about the board.

Devotion seiz'd the pair, to see the feast
With wine, and of no common grape, increas'd;
And up they held their hands, and fell to pray'r,
Excusing, as they could, their country fare.

"One goose they had, ('t was all they could allow,)
A wakeful sentry, and on duty now,
Whom to the gods for sacrifice they vow:
Her, with malicious zeal, the couple view'd;
She ran for life, and, limping, they pursued.
Full well the fowl perceiv'd their bad intent.
And would not make her masters' compliment;
But, persecuted, to the pow'rs she flies,
And close between the legs of Jove she lies.
He, with a gracious ear, the suppliant heard,
And sav'd her life; then what he was declar'd,
And own'd the god. 'The neighbourhood,' said he,
'Shall justly perish for impiety:
You stand alone exempted; but obey
With speed, and follow where we lead the way;
Leave these accurst, and to the mountain's height
Ascend, nor once look backward in your flight.'

"They haste, and what their tardy feet denied,
The trusty staff (their better leg) supplied.
An arrow's flight they wanted to the top,
And there secure, but spent with travel, stop;
Then turn their now no more forbidden eyes:
Lost in a lake the floated level lies;
A wat'ry desart covers all the plains;
Their cot alone, as in an aisle, remains;
Wond'ring with weeping eyes, while they deplore
Their neighbours' fate, and country now no more,
Their little shed, scarce large enough for two,
Seems, from the ground increas'd, in height and bulk to
     grow.
A stately temple shoots within the skies;
The crotches of their cot in columns rise;
The pavement polish'd marble they behold,
The gates with sculpture grac'd, the spires and tiles of gold.

"Then thus the Sire of Gods, with look serene:

'Speak thy desire, thou only just of men;
And thou, O woman, only worthy found
To be with such a man in marriage bound.'
  "A while they whisper; then, to Jove address'd,
Philemon thus prefers their joint request:
'We crave to serve before your sacred shrine,
And offer at your altars rites divine;
And since not any action of our life
Has been polluted with domestic strife,
We beg one hour of death; that neither she
With widow's tears may live to bury me,
Nor weeping I, with wither'd arms, may bear
My breathless Baucis to the sepulchre.'
  "The godheads sign their suit. They run their race
In the same tenor all th' appointed space;
Then, when their hour was come, while they relate
These past adventures at the temple gate,
Old Baucis is by old Philemon seen
Sprouting with sudden leaves of sprightly green;
Old Baucis look'd where old Philemon stood,
And saw his lengthen'd arms a sprouting wood.
New roots their fasten'd feet begin to bind,
Their bodies stiffen in a rising rind:
Then, ere the bark above their shoulders grew,
They give and take at once their last adieu;
At once: 'Farewell, O faithful spouse,' they said;
At once th' incroaching rinds their closing lips invade.
Ev'n yet, an ancient Tyanæan shows
A spreading oak, that near a linden grows;
The neighbourhood confirm the prodigy,
Grave men, not vain of tongue, or like to lie.
I saw myself the garlands on their boughs,
And tablets hung for gifts of granted vows;
And off'ring fresher up, with pious pray'r,
'The good,' said I, 'are God's peculiar care,
And such as honour Heav'n, shall heav'nly honour share.'"

All dreams, as in old Galen I have read,
Are from repletion and complexion bred;
From rising fumes of indigested food,
And noxious humours that infect the blood:
And sure, my lord, if I can read aright,
These foolish fancies you have had to-night
Are certain symptoms (in the canting style)
Of boiling choler, and abounding bile;
This yellow gall that in your stomach floats
Ingenders all these visionary thoughts.
When choler overflows, then dreams are bred
Of flames, and all the family of red;
Red dragons and red beasts in sleep we view,
For humours are distinguish'd by their hue.
From hence we dream of wars and warlike things,
And wasps and hornets with their double wings.

   Choler adust congeals our blood with fear;
Then black bulls toss us, and black devils tear.
In sanguine airy dreams aloft we bound,
With rheums oppress'd we sink in rivers drown'd.

   More I could say, but thus conclude my theme,
The dominating humour makes the dream.
Cato was in his time accounted wise,
And he condemns them all for empty lies.
Take my advice, and when we fly to ground,
With laxatives preserve your body sound,
And purge the peccant humours that abound.
I should be loth to lay you on a bier;
And tho' there lives no 'pothecary near,
I dare for once prescribe for your disease,
And save long bills, and a damn'd doctor's fees.

   Two sovereign herbs, which I by practice know,
And both at hand, (for in our yard they grow,)
On peril of my soul shall rid you wholly
Of yellow choler, and of melancholy:
You must both purge and vomit; but obey,
And for the love of heav'n make no delay.

G   ‡101‡

Since hot and dry in your complexion join,
Beware the sun when in a vernal sign;
For when he mounts exalted in the Ram,
If then he finds your body in a flame,
Replete with choler, I dare lay a groat,
A tertian ague is at least your lot.
Perhaps a fever (which the gods forefend!)
May bring your youth to some untimely end.
And therefore, sir, as you desire to live,
A day or two before your laxative,
Take just three worms, nor under nor above,
Because the gods unequal numbers love.
These digestives prepare you for your purge,
Of fumetery, centaury, and spurge;
And of ground-ivy add a leaf or two:
All which within our yard or garden grow.
Eat these, and be, my lord, of better cheer:
Your father's son was never born to fear.

* * * * * *

Dreams are but interludes which fancy makes;
When monarch Reason sleeps, this mimic wakes;
Compounds a medley of disjointed things,
A mob of cobblers, and a court of kings.
Light fumes are merry, grosser fumes are sad;
Both are the reasonable soul run mad:
And many monstrous forms in sleep we see,
That neither were, nor are, nor e'er can be.
Sometimes forgotten things long cast behind
Rush forward in the brain, and come to mind.
The nurse's legends are for truths receiv'd,
And the man dreams but what the boy believ'd.
Sometimes we but rehearse a former play;
The night restores our actions done by day,
As hounds in sleep will open for their prey.
In short the farce of dreams is of a piece,
Chimeras all; and more absurd, or less.

When Chanticleer the second watch had sung,
Scorning the scorner sleep, from bed I sprung;
And dressing, by the moon, in loose array,
Pass'd out in open air, preventing day,
And sought a goodly grove, as fancy led my way.
Straight as a line in beauteous order stood
Of oaks unshorn a venerable wood:
Fresh was the grass beneath; and ev'ry tree,
At distance planted in a due degree,
Their branching arms in air with equal space
Stretch'd to their neighbours with a long embrace;
And the new leaves on ev'ry bough were seen,
Some ruddy-colour'd, some of lighter green.
The painted birds, companions of the spring,
Hopping from spray to spray, were heard to sing;
Both eyes and ears receiv'd a like delight,
Enchanting music, and a charming sight.
On Philomel I fix'd my whole desire,
And listen'd for the queen of all the choir;
Fain would I hear her heav'nly voice to sing;
And wanted yet an omen to the spring.

Attending long in vain, I took the way,
Which thro' a path but scarcely printed lay;
In narrow mazes oft it seem'd to meet,
And look'd as lightly press'd by fairy feet.
Wand'ring I walk'd alone, for still me-thought
To some strange end so strange a path was wrought;
At last it led me where an arbour stood,
The sacred receptacle of the wood.
This place unmark'd, tho' oft I walk'd the green,
In all my progress I had never seen;
And, seiz'd at once with wonder and delight,
Gaz'd all around me, new to the transporting sight.
'T was bench'd with turf, and goodly to be seen,
The thick young grass arose in fresher green:
The mound was newly made, no sight could pass

Betwixt the nice partitions of the grass;
The well-united sods so closely lay,
And all around the shades defended it from day,
For sycamores with eglantine were spread,
A hedge about the sides, a covering over head.
And so the fragrant brier was wove between,
The sycamore and flow'rs were mix'd with green,
That nature seem'd to vary the delight,
And satisfied at once the smell and sight.
The master workman of the bow'r was known
Thro' fairy lands, and built for Oberon;
Who twining leaves with such proportion drew,
They rose by measure, and by rule they grew:
No mortal tongue can half the beauty tell,
For none but hands divine could work so well.
Both roof and sides were like a parlour made,
A soft recess, and a cool summer shade:
The hedge was set so thick, no foreign eye
The persons plac'd within it could espy;
But all that pass'd without with ease was seen,
As if nor fence nor tree was plac'd between.
'T was border'd with a field; and some was plain
With grass, and some was sow'd with rising grain,
That (now the dew with spangles deck'd the ground)
A sweeter spot of earth was never found.
I look'd and look'd, and still with new delight;
Such joy my soul, such pleasures fill'd my sight:
And the fresh eglantine exhal'd a breath,
Whose odours were of pow'r to raise from death.
Nor sullen discontent, nor anxious care,
Ev'n tho' brought thither, could inhabit there;
But thence they fled as from their mortal foe,
For this sweet place could only pleasure know.
   Thus, as I mus'd, I cast aside my eye,
And saw a medlar tree was planted nigh.
The spreading branches made a goodly show,
And full of opening blooms was ev'ry bough.
A goldfinch there I saw with gaudy pride
Of painted plumes, that hopp'd from side to side,

Still pecking as she pass'd; and still she drew
The sweets from ev'ry flow'r, and suck'd the dew:
Suffic'd at length, she warbled in her throat,
And tun'd her voice to many a merry note,
But indistinct, and neither sweet nor clear,
Yet such as sooth'd my soul and pleas'd my ear.
    Her short performance was no sooner tried,
When she I sought, the nightingale, replied:
So sweet, so shrill, so variously she sung,
That the grove echo'd, and the valleys rung;
And I so ravish'd with her heav'nly note,
I stood intranc'd, and had no room for thought,
But all o'erpow'r'd with ecstasy of bliss,
Was in a pleasing dream of Paradise.
At length I wak'd, and, looking round the bow'r,
Search'd ev'ry tree, and pried on ev'ry flow'r,
If anywhere by chance I might espy
The rural poet of the melody;
For still methought she sung not far away.
At last I found her on a laurel spray;
Close by my side she sate, and fair in sight,
Full in a line, against her opposite,
Where stood with eglantine the laurel twin'd,
And both their native sweets were well conjoin'd.
    On the green bank I sat, and listen'd long;
(Sitting was more convenient for the song!)
Nor till her lay was ended could I move,
But wish'd to dwell forever in the grove.
Only methought the time too swiftly pass'd,
And ev'ry note I fear'd would be the last.
My sight, and smell, and hearing were employ'd,
And all three senses in full gust enjoy'd.
And what alone did all the rest surpass,
The sweet possession of the fairy place;
Single, and conscious to myself alone
Of pleasures to th' excluded world unknown:
Pleasures which nowhere else were to be found,
And all Elysium in a spot of ground.

Imitated from Chaucer, and inlarg'd

A parish priest was of the pilgrim train;
An awful, reverend, and religious man.
His eyes diffus'd a venerable grace,
And charity itself was in his face.
Rich was his soul, tho' his attire was poor,
(As God had cloth'd his own ambassador;)
For such, on earth, his blest Redeemer bore.
Of sixty years he seem'd; and well might last
To sixty more, but that he liv'd too fast;
Refin'd himself to soul, to curb the sense;
And made almost a sin of abstinence.
Yet had his aspect nothing of severe,
But such a face as promis'd him sincere.
Nothing reserv'd or sullen was to see,
But sweet regards and pleasing sanctity;
Mild was his accent, and his action free.
With eloquence innate his tongue was arm'd;
Tho' harsh the precept, yet the preacher charm'd.
For, letting down the golden chain from high,
He drew his audience upward to the sky;
And oft, with holy hymns, he charm'd their ears
(A music more melodious than the spheres):
For David left him, when he went to rest,
His lyre, and after him he sung the best.
He bore his great commission in his look;
But sweetly temper'd awe, and soften'd all he spoke.
He preach'd the joys of heav'n and pains of hell,
And warn'd the sinner with becoming zeal,
But on eternal mercy lov'd to dwell.
He taught the gospel rather than the law,
And forc'd himself to drive, but lov'd to draw:
For fear but freezes minds; but love, like heat,
Exhales the soul sublime, to seek her native seat.
To threats the stubborn sinner oft is hard,
Wrapp'd in his crimes, against the storm prepar'd;
But, when the milder beams of mercy play,

He melts, and throws his cumbrous cloak away.
  Lightnings and thunder (heav'n's artillery)
As harbingers before th' Almighty fly:
Those but proclaim his style, and disappear;
The stiller sound succeeds, and God is there.
  The tithes his parish freely paid, he took;
But never sued, or curs'd with bell and book:
With patience bearing wrong, but off'ring none,
Since every man is free to lose his own.
The country churls, according to their kind,
(Who grudge their dues, and love to be behind,)
The less he sought his off'rings, pinch'd the more,
And prais'd a priest contented to be poor.
  Yet of his little he had some to spare,
To feed the famish'd, and to clothe the bare:
For mortified he was to that degree,
A poorer than himself he would not see.
True priests, he said, and preachers of the word,
Were only stewards of their sovereign Lord:
Nothing was theirs; but all the public store,
Intrusted riches, to relieve the poor;
Who, should they steal, for want of his relief,
He judg'd himself accomplice with the thief.
  Wide was his parish; not contracted close
In streets, but here and there a straggling house;
Yet still he was at hand, without request,
To serve the sick, to succour the distress'd;
Tempting, on foot, alone, without affright,
The dangers of a dark, tempestuous night.
  All this the good old man perform'd alone,
Nor spar'd his pains; for curate he had none.
Nor durst he trust another with his care;
Nor rode himself to Paul's, the public fair,
To chaffer for preferment with his gold,
Where bishoprics and sinecures are sold;
But duly watch'd his flock, by night and day,
And from the prowling wolf redeem'd the prey,
And hungry sent the wily fox away.
  The proud he tam'd, the penitent he cheer'd,

Nor to rebuke the rich offender fear'd.
His preaching much, but more his practice wrought;
(A living sermon of the truths he taught;)
For this by rules severe his life he squar'd,
That all might see the doctrine which they heard.
For priests, he said, are patterns for the rest;
(The gold of heav'n, who bear the God impress'd;)
But when the precious coin is kept unclean,
The sovereign's image is no longer seen.
If they be foul on whom the people trust,
Well may the baser brass contract a rust.

from CYMON AND IPHIGENIA [lines 399–408]

The country rings around with loud alarms,
And raw in fields the rude militia swarms;
Mouths without hands; maintain'd at vast expense,
In peace a charge, in war a weak defense:
Stout once a month they march, a blust'ring band,
And ever, but in times of need, at hand.
This was the morn when, issuing on the guard,
Drawn up in rank and file they stood prepar'd
Of seeming arms to make a short essay,
Then hasten to be drunk, the business of the day.

ON THE DEATH OF A VERY YOUNG GENTLEMAN

He who could view the book of destiny,
And read whatever there was writ of thee,
O *charming youth*, in the first op'ning page,
So many graces in so green an age,
Such wit, such modesty, such strength of mind,
A soul at once so manly, and so kind;
Would wonder, when he turn'd the volume o'er,
And after some few leaves should find no more,
Naught but a blank remain, a dead void space,
A step of life that promis'd such a race.

We must not, dare not think, that Heav'n began
A child, and could not finish him a man;
Reflecting what a mighty store was laid
Of rich materials, and a model made;
The cost already furnish'd; so bestow'd,
As more was never to one soul allow'd:
Yet after this profusion spent in vain,
Nothing but mold'ring ashes to remain.
I guess not, lest I split upon the shelf,
Yet durst I guess, Heav'n kept it for himself;
And giving us the use, did soon recall,
Ere we could spare, the mighty principal.

Thus then he disappear'd, was rarified;
For 't is improper speech to say he died:
He was exhal'd; his great Creator drew
His spirit, as the sun the morning dew.
'T is sin produces death; and he had none,
But the taint Adam left on ev'ry son.
He added not, he was so pure, so good,
'T was but th' original forfeit of his blood;
And that so little, that the river ran
More clear than the corrupted fount began.
Nothing remain'd of the first muddy clay;
The length of course had wash'd it in the way:
So deep, and yet so clear, we might behold
The gravel bottom, and that bottom gold.

As such we lov'd, admir'd, almost ador'd,
Gave all the tribute mortals could afford.
Perhaps we gave so much, the pow'rs above
Grew angry at our superstitious love;
For when we more than human homage pay,
The charming cause is justly snatch'd away.

Thus was the crime not his, but ours alone;
And yet we murmur that he went so soon,
Tho' miracles are short and rarely shown.

Hear then, ye mournful parents, and divide
That love in many, which in one was tied.
That individual blessing is no more,
But multiplied in your remaining store.

The flame 's dispers'd, but does not all expire;
The sparkles blaze, tho' not the globe of fire.
Love him by parts, in all your num'rous race,
And from those parts form one collected grace;
Then, when you have refin'd to that degree,
Imagine all in one, and think that one is he.

THE SECULAR MASQUE, *from* THE PILGRIM

[*Enter* JANUS.

   Janus.

Chronos, Chronos, mend thy pace;
   An hundred times the rolling sun
   Around the radiant belt has run
In his revolving race.
Behold, behold, the goal in sight;
Spread thy fans, and wing thy flight.

[*Enter* CHRONOS, *with a scythe in his hand, and a great globe on his back, which he sets down at his entrance.*

   Chronos.

Weary, weary of my weight,
Let me, let me, drop my freight,
   And leave the world behind.
I could not bear
Another year
   The load of humankind.

[*Enter* MOMUS, *laughing.*

   Momus.

Ha! ha! ha! ha! ha! ha! well hast thou done
   To lay down thy pack,
   And lighten thy back;
The world was a fool, e'er since it begun,
And since neither Janus, nor Chronos, nor I
   Can hinder the crimes,
   Or mend the bad times,
'T is better to laugh than to cry.
   Chorus of all Three.
   'T is better to laugh than to cry.

Janus.

Since Momus comes to laugh below,
    Old Time, begin the show,
That he may see, in every scene,
What changes in this age have been.

Chronos.

Then, goddess of the silver bow, begin.

[*Horns, or hunting music within.*

[*Enter* DIANA.

Diana.

With horns and with hounds I waken the day.
And hie to my woodland walks away;
I tuck up my robe, and am buskin'd soon,
And tie to my forehead a wexing moon.
I course the fleet stag, unkennel the fox,
And chase the wild goats o'er summits of rocks;
With shouting and hooting we pierce thro' the sky,
And Echo turns hunter, and doubles the cry.

Chorus of All.

With shouting and hooting we pierce thro' the sky,
And Echo turns hunter, and doubles the cry.

Janus.

Then our age was in its prime:

Chronos.

Free from rage:

Diana.

    And free from crime:

Momus.

A very merry, dancing, drinking,
Laughing, quaffing, and unthinking time.

Chorus of All.

Then our age was in its prime,
Free from rage, and free from crime;
A very merry, dancing, drinking,
Laughing, quaffing, and unthinking time.

[*Dance of* DIANA's *attendants.*

[*Enter* Mars.

Mars.

Inspire the vocal brass, inspire;
The world is past its infant age:
Arms and honour,
Arms and honour,
Set the martial mind on fire,
And kindle manly rage.
Mars has look'd the sky to red;
And Peace, the lazy good, is fled.
Plenty, Peace, and Pleasure fly;
The sprightly green
In woodland walks no more is seen;
The sprightly green has drunk the Tyrian dye.

Chorus of All.

Plenty, Peace, &c.

Mars.

Sound the trumpet, beat the drum;
Thro' all the world around,
Sound a reveille, sound, sound,
The warrior god is come.

Chorus of All.

Sound the trumpet, &c.

Momus.

Thy sword within the scabbard keep,
And let mankind agree;
Better the world were fast asleep,
Than kept awake by thee.
The fools are only thinner,
With all our cost and care;
But neither side a winner,
For things are as they were.

Chorus of All.

The fools are only, &c.

[*Enter* Venus.

Venus.

Calms appear when storms are past,
Love will have his hour at last:

Nature is my kindly care;
Mars destroys, and I repair;
Take me, take me, while you may;
Venus comes not ev'ry day.

Chorus of All.

 Take her, take her, &c.

Chronos.

The world was then so light,
I scarcely felt the weight;
Joy rul'd the day, and Love the night.
But since the Queen of Pleasure left the ground,
  I faint, I lag,
  And feebly drag
The pond'rous orb around.

Momus.

All, all of a piece throughout:

[*Pointing to* DIANA.

Thy chase had a beast in view;

[*To* MARS.

Thy wars brought nothing about;

[*To* VENUS.

Thy lovers were all untrue.

Janus.

'T is well an old age is out:

Chronos.

And time to begin a new.

Chorus of All.

 All, all of a piece throughout:
 Thy chase had a beast in view;
 Thy wars brought nothing about;
 Thy lovers were all untrue.
 'T is well an old age is out,
 And time to begin a new.

[*Dance of huntsmen, nymphs, warriors, and lovers.*

INDEX OF FIRST LINES

(*Note*: * indicates the first lines of extracts from longer poems which are not necessarily the opening lines of the poems themselves.)